TOUCHED BY THE
FIRE OF GOD

BY
JEFF LACKI

TATE PUBLISHING, LLC

ISBN: 1-59886-11-6-6

Purpose

In writing this book, I will give my own testimony as well as do some teaching on the Word of God. My testimony is, of course, my own. The teaching of the Word is based on what God has shown me and done with me during these last few years after I became a born again Christian. I realize that God is constantly working in our lives to teach us and change us. That said, this book is not without error. That is to say, I'm teaching on what I know today to be true. Since God's wisdom is infinite and our wisdom is finite, I don't assume to know everything about every topic, nor even come close. I can say that most of what you read is probably the absolute truth, but I also encourage you to seek the Lord if there is anything that I say or teach that doesn't sit right with you. This book is not intended to put anyone off or to mislead anyone in the body of Christ or turn people away from God. We are all brothers and sisters in the Lord. I humbly submit this to you, the reader, and ask that you take from this book the parts that are relevant to your own life and experiences in Him. I hope this book encourages and strengthens your walk with Him.

If you are an unbeliever, this book will also encourage you to know more about our Lord and Savior, Jesus Christ. It will show through my own life how real God is and how much He cares for each person He has created, believer or unbeliever. The Lord is always trying to get the attention of those who do not believe through life's circumstances and trials. I hope you hear

His call, open the door of your heart, and receive Jesus Christ into your life as your personal savior.

Dedication

I'm dedicating this book first and foremost to the one whom all glory and honor belongs, our Lord and Savior Jesus Christ, without which I would not have this testimony or book of what He has done for me and in my life.

Secondly, I dedicate this book to my God given, wonderful loving family, Larry, Leona, Michael and his wife Maralee Lacki. Without your raising me and supporting me in God's love all these years, I would not be the person I am today.

I would also like to dedicate this to my wonderful friends who God led me to after I was saved. To this day, they remain my closest brothers and sisters in Christ and ministry.

To Mike and Janet Yrigoyen, John Duarte, Parker Kurtz, Shelly Laden, Adam Stacci, Peter Soule', Frank Giordanno and Pastor Varkey and his family. We shared awesome moments and countless times together in the Lord's presence. They will forever be special moments in each of our lives.

And last but not least, to the couple who God used here in Arizona to instill within me the power of God in a way I had never known, my good friends Ron and Anita Heyn.

I love you all very much!

Contents

Foreword. 9

Introduction. 11

Growing up as a Catholic 15

Saved by an Angel 19

My Rebellion 23

How did I get here?. 41

The Lord is Real! 63

Years of Hardship 69

Count the Cost 103

Forgiveness. 115

The Lord's Return is Near. 123

Faith 133

Finances 149

Sex and Sexual Purity. 153

Other Testimonies. 169

Other Prophetic Words 175

"It is Finished" 183

Conclusion 195

Salvation Prayer 199

Foreword

Jeff Lacki has written a most unusual personal autobiography growing up as a Catholic, how the Lord brought about his salvation, and how He has been working in his life ever since.

"Touched by the Fire of God" is a beautiful story of how God has changed him over the years. He makes it very plain in a very unique way that the Christian life is not always smooth that there are some bumps along the road that you encounter, but how he surmounted those is told in a very beautiful, exciting way.

Reading this book will change your life in many ways if you are willing to let it, and we sincerely recommend it.

Charles and Frances Hunter
Authors, *How to Heal the Sick*

Introduction

When I first became a born again Christian, I had no idea the path that God was about to take me upon. My immediate and extended family thought that I had gotten involved in a cult because I was so different all of a sudden. Even Jesus was not taken well when He went into His own hometown. **"And they took offense at him. But Jesus said to them, 'Only in his hometown and in his own house is a prophet without honor'"** **(Matthew 13:57).** Obviously I was not and currently am not a prophet; however, the statement is valid for each of us who become believers. It is those who know us best that often find it hardest to believe what we now have come to believe in Christ. After all, they grew up with us or knew us in a very close manner, and here we have become changed quite quickly from what we used to be to what we are now becoming in Christ.

As I started writing this book I had no idea what form or shape it would take. All I knew was the Lord began speaking to my heart to write down all that He has shown me and done in my life, and that it would encourage and help others by my own testimony. I had some ideas of how I wanted it to be, but in the end it is the Holy Spirit that wrote this book. I've always held books in higher regard that talk about real life testimonies and experiences with God more than those that just teach. Neither is more important; I feel both are very valuable. My personality lends itself better to testimony rather than teaching, even though I enjoy teaching the Bible. To know personally someone whose life has been changed or influenced by the power of God brings home the truth of the Bible beyond the words of the Bible. Ultimately, the Bible *is* the most important book however. Jesus himself in the Gospels often told people to "Go and tell how much God has done for you." I firmly believe that testimony of what God has done for an individual is something that the church in America is lacking in these last days. It's harder to believe what happened in the Bible thousands of years ago. How much more powerful it is when someone we know or hear about has a real life testimony of what the Living God has done for them consistent with His Word, the Bible in the here and now?

I hope by writing this book to show another powerful testimony of the living God. I also hope to demonstrate God's awesome power through Jesus Christ, which continues to change me and sanctify me day by day. Even while writing this book, God has done some amazing things that I had been praying about for years. I will share them later as you read on. In the last 7 years, God has poured Himself into me. I hope that my own testimony in this book reveals His love, His power, and His great and awesome grace and mercy for others who may not yet know Him. To those who already know Him, to encourage and edify the Body of Christ, even in the midst of their deepest trials. I also hope to show that God has a plan for each and every person born (Jeremiah 29:11, Psalm 139:16) by giving my own testimony of God's work in me thus far. Every life is a gift of God and from God. Every person born has the choice of heaven or hell, to do good or evil in any and every circumstance in his or her lives. Which will you choose? I encourage you to read on and see just one man's testimony of God's miraculous life-changing power through Jesus Christ.

During the course of the book and testimony, I have put several prophetic words from the Lord within the text to encourage you and reveal what God was saying to me at the various meetings. These words were given either to me personally from the Lord, or to a group of us at different prayer meetings. Each one was recorded as the word came forth through the prophet and was later transcribed. I must pause a moment and explain. The prophetic gift in the Bible does not always have to do with foretelling the future, although this is certainly a part of the gifting. It is also used as God speaks through someone to an individual or group of people as the person is carried along by the Holy Spirit to speak God's heart for the question or matter that God's dealing with. Sometimes God's own joy over what was said or done in the meeting brought forth a word to us. There are examples of this in Jeremiah and other books. **"Jesus Christ is the same yesterday and today and forever" (Hebrews 13:8).** God's ways never change, yet because people have not experienced something, I've noticed they are often quick to dismiss its reality or existence when it comes to things of God. Without going into great teaching or detail, the prophetic gift is mentioned in 1Corinthians chapters 12–14. Any prophetic word will never go against what the Bible teaches. Most, if not all of the prophetic words contained in this book, have portions that you can directly point to in scripture. I encourage you to read what the Bible says about it, and how it is a gift that the Lord says even to pray for.

If at anytime during the reading of this book you yourself would like to receive eternal salvation, it's as easy as the prayer on page 199. I should also note that anytime I say "Satan" or enemy, my reference is of Satan's kingdom and the demons assigned to the evil tasks against me or the body of Christ. Satan is not omnipresent and does not have the time to personally visit most of the saints to work at their destruction. Instead, he assigns these tasks to his demons under him, which are constantly at work. **"The thief comes only to steal and kill and destroy; I have come that they may have life, and have it to the full" (John 10:10).**

May God bless you and as you read this book.

Growing Up as A Catholic

I was born in October, 1966 on the south side of Chicago, a small suburb a few blocks from the city. We were a Catholic family who attended mass each week for the most part. My parents were hard working middle class people who loved both my brother and me very much and tried to do their best in raising us. My brother had L.D. (learning disability), A.D.D. (Attention deficit disorder) and hyperactivity. He was a handful for my parents. I am about 2 years older than he. I on the other hand was a quiet, reserved child who listened to authority and did what I was told. I rarely got into any serious trouble. My brother on the other hand was constantly being scolded or disciplined for something. He and I were on opposite ends of the spectrum. It's probably why we both fought constantly.

Those years seem a lifetime ago, and they really are at the age of 38. I didn't always understand why we went to church or what it was about when I was younger. I was just bored to tears and happy to get out of there each week. My parents made us go and honestly, I had no idea why, like most children. As I got older it was just something we did every Sunday. We put our "time in" on the weekends and the rest of the week was "ours." I say that because I had no idea of the things of God at that time, like most young people. Your environment at that age usually dictates what you believe or don't believe, and what you do and don't do. To be honest, I hated going to church when I was younger. I looked at it as a necessary evil in my life to please my parents and God, the little I knew Him or of Him. Even so, in some very small way I felt good inside about doing it once a week, even though I really didn't want to attend. It was as if I did my duty by going.

Just a couple years ago, my mother told me a story about when I was 6 yrs old. Interestingly enough, I have memories as young as two. Much of my childhood I can remember with amazing clarity even to this day. I have a bit of a photographic memory, and I can still "see" things of my childhood as if I am still there. My mother told me of a time when I was telling her that angels were visiting me and telling me that I was going to die soon. This was a time where my father and mother were attending Christian prayer meetings on a weekly basis. We had a neighbor who was a born again Christian, and even though my parents were Catholic, they still attended these meetings on a regular basis. I don't recall any of this now, but the story continues that my mother was, to say the least, terrified. She told me she prayed that if this was truly God's will that He would give her peace, comfort and strength to get through it. She said the most incredible peace and love came over her, something she cannot fully describe, but she knew it was the Lord. Obviously nothing ever happened to me, which leads me to my next story. One night after we (my mother, brother and I) came home from dinner (my father was working second shift as a printer), I went upstairs to my attic bedroom. There was a man standing in the closet. To this day I can still see this man standing there. Funny thing was, he was short–short enough that he fit under the shelf that usually hangs above the clothes bar in a closet. I don't recall him speaking a word to me, nor I to him. I went downstairs and told my mother. Of course she was terrified, not sure if she should call the police or if I was making this up. She grabbed the broom and led the way upstairs and checked out the place...nothing. The man had vanished.

I've read many Christian books on demons and deliverance and was part of a deliverance ministry for a few years as well. Based on this experience, I believe that "imaginary childhood friends" are very often, if not always, demons.

The Bible says that **"Satan himself masquerades as an angel of light" (2Corinthians 11:14),** so we know he and his demons can appear to be real people or even "angels." **"Do not forget to entertain strangers, for by so doing some people have entertained angels without knowing it" (Hebrews 13:2).** Just as angels appeared to Mary and others in the Bible, so demons can appear to us. After all, demons are just fallen angels and still retain powers until the end when God judges them. **"For I am convinced that neither death nor life, neither angels nor demons, neither the present nor the future, nor any powers, neither height nor depth, nor anything else in all creation, will be able to separate us from the love of God that is in Christ Jesus our Lord" (Romans 8:38–39).** I'm unsure why they appear to some and not others, but they do appear. Children have no pre-conceived ideas of right and wrong. Children will also believe nearly anything you tell them. Some children are lonely and in need of a friend, either by neglect, abuse or other circumstances. Demons are always happy to oblige. My experience as a child does not fit into either category. I've often wondered if it was a demon testing me out to see if I would communicate with it or not. I won't know until I die and the Lord reveals it to me. The fact remains, it was indeed a demon.

My life was somewhat normal and typical. I played street football, baseball, and hide and seek with my friends–the few I had. Life was always hard at school for me, not because I didn't learn and do ok, but because I was always picked on and wouldn't defend myself. The Lord showed me recently even how those experiences have prepared me for the ministry I'm about to step into in the days ahead. As I've grown in Him, the fear of man has left me more and more, and the boldness in Christ has come forth. Where once I was shy and timid, now I am bold and don't care so much what others are thinking of me, because I know Him and who I am in Christ. He is the one who defines who I am, not the world or other people. My faith has deepened to the point now where when I share, there's not the embarrassment of Jesus, but the boldness of Jesus within me. I truly know what I stand for and how real He is. As I stand on the Word of God, I know what I speak to be true when I'm witnessing to someone. Where once I was blind, now I see clearly. **"But their minds were made dull, for to this day the same veil remains when the old covenant is read. It has not been removed, because only in Christ is it taken away. Even to this day when Moses is read, a veil covers their hearts. But whenever anyone turns to the Lord, the veil is taken away" (2Corinthians 3:14–16).** Each day, that clarity grows more and more as I grow in the Lord.

Saved by An Angel

Skipping forward to the age of 19–I had graduated high school the year before and had had a spontaneous lung collapse known as a spontaneous pneumothorax. It nearly killed me as I later found out. I had had minor chest pains, and pain in both my left arm and neck on and off for a couple years in high school. The pains always seemed to go away after a couple days on their own. I spent 3 weeks in the hospital that Christmas. What a bummer that was, and the days before cable TV was everywhere. I was bored out of my mind at that cold December hospital. I had 3 chest tubes during two different stays that month. The first was the emergency one. I stayed four days in the hospital and then was released. One week later I had some minor chest pain. They re-admitted me for fluid buildup in the chest cavity and had to insert two more chest tubes at two different times during my stay. I didn't know during that time the doctors had no idea what kind of viral infection I had and were expecting me to die because they didn't know how to effectively treat it. I felt perfectly fine, though entirely bored and wanting to go home.

About one year after that experience, I got a job with my mom working for a law firm in downtown Chicago. We took the train downtown everyday and had to walk about nine blocks to get through the city to work. One morning I stood on a corner of a one-way street. I was at the curb, the first one ready to go when the light changed, with about 30 people crowded behind me. As I often did, I checked for traffic in the direction of the one-way street and seeing that it was clear, decided to start off the curb against the "Do not Walk" light. I no sooner picked up my foot and began to shift my weight forward when a man grabbed me by the jacket (it was December and cold) and promptly pulled me back. It was a shock to me to say the least, so much so I was offended and started to turn around and say, "What the heck . . ." when immediately a bus that was traveling by in the opposite direction in the very lane of traffic I was about to step into drove by at about 15 miles per hour. Granted this isn't fast; however, with the amount of weight of that bus, I would have gone flying probably 100 feet if I had been struck, and more than likely killed. My heart sank. Instead of being mad about being held back, I curtly said "thanks" to whomever was behind me. The light then changed and we started walking again. My mother had been standing behind me someplace and saw it happen but didn't remember the man at all afterward. After all, her son nearly just died in front of her!

I tell that story because in the couple years before I became a Christian, my mother had given me a book on angel stories. They were amazing stories of people being saved where there was no way, other than angelic intervention, that their lives were saved. I thought back to my own life and if there was ever a time when an angel may have saved me. I realized there was, and I realized as far as I could tell, that "man" had been an angel sent by the Lord to save my life, presumably because God's plan for my life was and is not yet fulfilled. Not only my physical life, but very possibly my spiritual life as well. God can only know for sure. I also believe it was an angel because there was no way anyone could have acted so quickly to hold me back. I had barely even gotten my foot off the ground to move when I was held back. No one except God could have known I was about to step off that curb and react so quickly to save me.

Shortly after that, my health insurance through my parents was going to expire unless I became a full time college student again. At the last minute I enrolled at Southern Illinois University at Carbondale in the electronics program. My first semester at college was hard. Being so shy, I didn't meet too many people easily. I was also stuck on the worst floor in the dorms at the area where I lived. It was rowdy, loud and obnoxious. I rarely stayed up there if I was out of my room at all. I remember sitting quietly many nights watching television on my little black and white alone on the weekends. That first semester was very difficult for me. I really missed what was familiar to me. I had never been away from home like that before, on my own. I was quite happy to go home that coming summer. I did meet my future roommate that first semester and we remained roommates through the end of college.

Later that summer I went on a 500 mile bicycle trip across Illinois to raise money for the American Lung Association. By that fall, I was a little more excited to go back and room with someone that I knew rather than someone I was stuck with, even though God had mercy on me and gave me a decent roommate that first semester. He went home every weekend, which was nice for me. Now that my second semester was underway, college started becoming fun, to a degree. I moved down to the first floor of the same dorm. Guys on the new floor I moved to were amazed I didn't drink at all, so of course they started pressuring me to have beer and drink. I did, but at first I hated it. I remember one of my "friends" in college forcing me to steal a glass pitcher (half full of beer no less, and right under a group of people's noses!) with him at a bar one night. I was so nervous, but I did it because I was forced to. To this day, I'm amazed they didn't chase after us or notice we took it as we walked out the back door with a glass pitcher and about 8 glasses. Again, it was God's protection. Even though I wasn't technically saved yet, He was with me. Another time at a party, my "friends" decided they wanted this couch off the back porch of the house we were at. We carried the couch down several blocks, across a busy street, and all the way across campus at about 2am without getting caught. I'm still amazed at God's protection over the stupid evil things I did in my life, which compared with many today are "child's play" I'm sure, as the evil around us intensifies with each passing day.

Our campus also had a small forest section that divided Thompson point, where I lived in the dorms, with the main campus area. A couple small trails led through the generally dark forest. We often had to walk through the forest at night to get uptown to the bars and clubs. I remember walking through there many times alone and praying for safety. In my 4 years at college walking through those woods, I never once had a problem; however, there were many reported rapes and robberies in those same woods. Just luck, or God's protection? I already know the answer.

Jeff Lacki

My Rebellion

My life has always been very lonely. Being introverted and shy, I didn't go out much or participate in much of anything. When I was in grammar school I never had more than two friends. I was constantly picked on and teased for my looks, my last name–whatever kids could find, they found and exploited. I was timid and shy, which didn't help any. On top of that, I wasn't very good at sports when I was younger. I was always picked last when teams were chosen. Really the kids didn't want to pick me at all, but were forced to because of the P.E. class or whatever. Kids are very cruel. Satan loves to use children to hurt other children. We see it everyday. You don't need to teach a child how to cheat or lie. You do, however, need to teach a child the way of the Lord. This is due to the fall of man in the Garden of Eden of course. It's why we all need a savior in Jesus Christ, because we live in a cursed and fallen world.

On top of the general abuse at school in childhood, I didn't know of any girls who liked me, at least romantically. Well, this wasn't entirely true. There were a few, but they tended to be the ones that I just had no interest in at all. I never dated anyone. I was very shy, reserved and an introvert, but deep inside I was crying out for attention and love from someone of the opposite sex. I desperately wanted to date someone. As I got older, my desire was not only to date but marry someone special, like most people.

In college I finally got a chance to interact with the opposite sex. Coming from an all boys Catholic high school really put a damper on my social growth with women. My shyness didn't help one bit. I was very naive in some ways and had a lot of growing up to do. I was also shocked by the fact that everyone around me was pretty much having sex left and right. This was back in the late 1980s. I can imagine how much worse it is in schools today. It bothered me deeply. Not only did I think I was entirely ugly because nobody seemed to like me, but also I felt that premarital sex was morally wrong. Some may say I was idealistic, but I really wanted to marry a virgin. All I saw around me were young men and women who weren't and didn't care about waiting for someone special to have sex with. They'd give themselves away to anyone who wanted a little fun. It really bothered me and hurt me at the time. Little did I realize just how much.

I remember thinking I must be the ugliest guy around. What made things worse for me was that if I was so ugly, I didn't have the usual things that people tend to say about ugly people. I wasn't fat. I didn't have any physical deformities–nothing. I was tall and in my eyes, very average minimally. Also, please don't misunderstand me–fat people or physically challenged people are also God's creation. Their reward is probably far more than my own. I'm just sharing how I felt at that time. I saw no worldly reason that nobody seemed to like me, and I was very depressed inside. That depression started leading to thoughts of suicide. I'd also like to add that just because we see someone's exterior and think they are attractive or ugly, it has no bearing on what the reality that they live each and every day may be. I've since been told by many women that I am handsome, cute, whatever the case may be. I've also learned that just because someone seems to be something does not mean they necessarily have those things in their real day to day life. I apparently had a lot going for me and have not had the normal things like a girlfriend(s) for years now. The good part of that is that I know why now. God has been protecting me for His plans and purposes all this time. If I had had the things I wanted back then, I probably would have been the type of guy who slept around and did those other worldly things. I thank God I didn't do those things now!

My college friends and roommates and I used to go exploring all over the woods of southern Illinois near school. I bought myself a large hunting knife once as a "just in case" to have when we would go out. One night in my dorm room while my roommate was gone for the weekend, I remember sitting in the dark and listening to my stereo. I was sitting in a recliner we had and wondering what it would be like to plunge that knife into my stomach. I was feeling quite lonely and depressed as I so very often did by that time in my life. I remember hearing what I thought was my own voice, but I know now was Satan's voice. "Go ahead...do it... plunge it into yourself nice and hard. Who will miss you? Who will care? Nobody cares about you. Everyone thinks your ugly...you aren't popular, you aren't ANYBODY." I had heard that voice many times during college and had always thought it was just some fleeting thought. Probably the biggest reason I didn't do it was that I loved my parents and family so much, and I couldn't hurt them like that. While my pain was so real and so deep, the pain I would inflict on them would be far worse. I sat in my dorm room many times, alone in the dark, wanting to cry, but couldn't for whatever reason. I believe that is also why I am somewhat of an overachiever. I received nearly straight As in college, compared to high school where I was an average C-B student. Many semesters I pulled off 4.0 GPAs. If I was getting a C, I considered it failing. My parents weren't on me about my grades ever; it was all me. I was on myself for the fact that nobody, outside my family, truly cared about me, and I wanted to be somebody. This is probably why I have been told by some people that I seem to be able to do just about anything. I always strived to learn more about how to do things, how things worked, trying to become a black belt and a pilot, etc. I don't do those things now to try to be someone. I only do what I do now because I either like doing it or it pleases God.

There was a young woman, a freshman, who showed interest in me my senior year of college. She wasn't what I really wanted, but at that point I was so desperate and so devastated that nobody had ever wanted me all through college that I decided to date her. We only dated for two weeks before I just couldn't handle it. I didn't want to lead her on, and I also wasn't that interested in her. I felt guilty. I remember how bad I felt the night I told her I wanted to end it, and that was only a two week relationship. At the age of 23, I finally had my first kiss. I felt again like such a failure and a big-time loser. Again, Satan's plans were working in my life to keep me down and oppressed rather than free as Christ wanted me to be. But I had no idea of these things because nobody ever told me about Jesus and a personal relationship with Him, not even the Catholic Church.

The summer I graduated from college with a B.S. degree in electronics, I moved to Silicon Valley in San Jose, California to find work. My cousin invited me to come live with him and his roommate until I found a

Jeff Lacki

job. Interestingly, I had always wanted to go to Phoenix, Arizona after college because I really liked it there the one time my family visited in 1984. So in July, 1990, I packed up my pickup truck and headed to California. I didn't find any electronic jobs until January, 1991. Instead I worked at Mervyn's during those first several months in California. I was depressed yet again. I had a great college degree, I had graduated Cum Laude, and here I was making $5.35/hour at Mervyn's. What was going on? I remember having as little as $0.52 in my banking account some weeks. It got so bad for me that I seriously considered returning home to Chicago. My parents missed me a lot and kept putting thoughts in my head about not making it, and "what will you do if..." etc. I went back and forth in my mind about staying or returning home. I must have had a moment of weakness one night at Mervyn's because I remember deciding that I would return home to Chicago as I left the store after work one night. I called my parents and told them. They immediately booked a plane ticket for my brother to fly out and drive home with me in 2 weeks. During that two week period, I had another revelation. If I returned home to Chicago, I would always wonder what could have been if I had stayed. I had wanted to live out west all of my life. It was almost harder to return than to stay. About 1 week later, I called my parents back and told them I was not going to come home. I couldn't live with myself if I had given up. As hard as it was to stay, I was staying. My parents were very upset with me, I think more than any other time in my life. Looking back, I think they were more upset due to selfish reasons than not. I had given them what they wanted, which was me returning home, then taken it back a week later. My brother's plane ticket was a round-trip ticket because it was cheaper, so he came and visited us for several days and returned home.

My cousin was making good money and was helping me pay rent. That time seemed to drag on and on forever. About that same time, November 1990, the gulf war buildup was already underway and the economy took a nose dive. By the end of January 1991, I had somehow managed to get interviews at two different high tech companies out of the blue at the same time! I took the one paying the most amount of money. It was also the most interesting job of the two as well. I started working at Megatest building chip test equipment, which was sold to chip manufacturing companies around the world. For the first time since college nearly 9 months earlier, I felt great again–at least on the outside.

Just after getting my new "high paying" job, I decided to do something I had always wanted to do, probably because I always felt like a nobody. I signed up with the local Tae Kwon Do studio. It started to give me the confidence I had been looking for all those years, as well as getting my body into excellent physical shape. I almost didn't sign up at first. As I drove up to the studio the first day, there were so many people coming and going, and the place was so small, that it was very intimidating. I nearly turned around and went home, I had so much fear. I really don't know why, except that I have always been a very shy person around people I don't know. This was very intimidating, and yet I knew that if I turned around, I would never overcome my fear or fears by running away from them.

About 3 years later at the age of 27, I was in the middle of my training in Tae Kwon Do. I was a purple belt at the time, about half way to my black belt. It was during this time that I started chatting online much more than I had in previous years. I was promoted to software engineer 2 years earlier and had first starting chatting online when I was in college before the internet really took off. I would go into chat rooms and meet single women online. Inevitably, the conversations would turn to relationships and sometimes sexual things. I was a pretty naïve person at the age of 27 even after college. I had never had sex before, let alone a real girlfriend. I had tried a dating service once, which is something I'd never do again. Again, girls I wasn't interested in seemed to like me. I wasn't good at blowing people off, for whatever reason, so I blew off the dating service. Being 27 and never having a girlfriend yet was bothering me more and more. During college, all my friends were out sleeping around for the most part. I was a very good "moral" person. I believe now that God protected me from understanding those things to protect me for His future plans and purposes for my life. I had no idea just how much sexual activity was going on all around me, even more than what I thought I knew of in college. My parents never sheltered me. It was just that by my own personality, I had sheltered myself by being shy and not going out much, even in college.

As I talked with these younger girls, basically 17–28 or so, I realized that nearly 95% of them had already had sex at least once, if not multiple times with multiple guys. Some even had children already and were unwed. I had always wanted to marry a virgin. Don't ask me why, but it was part of who I was, I guess. I knew that I was a virgin and wanted the same. It was something very special to me in my heart. I started to get angry. The more girls I talked with, the angrier I became inside, and that anger started turning towards God. I had prayed since I was 6 or 7 years old for a girlfriend in my life, nearly daily. Here I was–27 years old, a virgin–and just about every girl I met, both in real life and on the internet, was not a virgin. Besides that, nobody seemed interested in me still. What was wrong with me? Even as my confidence in myself grew in martial arts, my inward confidence in whom I was and if people liked me seemed to be sinking further. Anger and hatred were building up deep within me, and I didn't quite realize it yet.

My anger grew and grew until I went down to Arizona to visit my cousin for a week on a vacation. I had met a girl online who seemed to like me and it was a good excuse to meet her, plus my parents were going to Arizona as well for a small vacation. Her and I met and went out one night. I really liked her, and she seemed to really like me as well. We had tentative plans to go out another night when she called me back and said she couldn't make it. She told me that this guy she knew from school (she attended a community college) invited her to spend the night at his place because his parents were going out of town. She said we could go out after she spent the two days with him. She also told me, or it came out, that she was going to have sex with him. It was at that moment the anger that had been building inside of me for years over being single and watching everyone in the world around me date, have sex and not be lonely brewed to the top. I was full of jealousy, envy and rage. I snapped. My parents had come down from Chicago to visit Phoenix the day before. There was a misunderstanding between myself and my cousin that came to a head also. With the situation with this girl, I just lost it inside. I told my parents

I was leaving that evening after only seeing them for one day. I felt really bad about only seeing them for one day, but my inner wounded-ness was more than I could bear. I didn't tell them anything about this girl, only just that the situation with my cousin was why I was leaving. Now it was an 11 hour trip back to San Jose by car. I had driven my brand new jeep down without a top, and it was 5pm when I left Phoenix in October. I remember freezing my butt off all the way home, on top of fighting sleep. I just didn't care. I was so mad, so upset, so hurt, so angry at this girl I cared about. But really it was more at God and the years of my life that seemed to never amount to anything in the direction I wanted it to go. Part of me didn't care if I ran off the road and died, or someone hit me with their car and I died. Life was meaningless being alone, and I didn't think I could take it much longer.

I made it home safely at about 5am. I was about half-way to getting my black belt and decided that I would pursue my job and training full time from then on. After all, I had nothing else to live for at the moment. I was lonely, angry, and my desires for some-one that I didn't have yet in my life were consuming me. I blew that girl off completely in Arizona. I told her that if she really liked me, she sure didn't care too much by what she did. I remember getting into some heavy metal music more than I had before. I started getting the attitude that I was going to go out and sleep with as many women as I could from then on and enjoy life the way I wanted to live, like everyone else seemed to be doing around me. I would not do what I thought God wanted me to do, or even what my "moral" inner voice was telling me was right and wrong. I decided that God must not exist. My logic was such that I had prayed for 22 years for a girlfriend and then a wife every night, and the prayer had apparently fallen on deaf ears. Therefore, God is not real and He never existed. The problem was that deep inside me, I knew there was a God. I can't explain it, but this small part of me still believed. The bigger part of me kept stuffing that voice out because I just couldn't deal with the loneliness and the pain another day. The Bible says **"I will put my law in their minds and write it on their hearts. I will be their God, and they will be my people. No longer will a man teach his neighbor, or a man his brother saying, 'Know the Lord,' because they will all know me, from the least of them to the greatest, declares the Lord" (Jeremiah 31:34).**

I believe many people out there, maybe even reading this book, hear that same small voice. God is whispering to you as he did to Elijah in **1Kings19:12 "And after the fire came a gentle whisper."** I would encourage you to listen to that voice. It is the voice of the Living God speaking to your heart. No matter what has happened to you or what you've been through, Jesus has never left you. The reason He has allowed bad things in your life is not to punish you or harm you, but to use you and bless you once you to turn your life to Him. It's also happened because you haven't given Him back what was His to begin with–your life. Once you give your life to Jesus and trust in Him alone, nothing from that point on happens to you by chance, good or bad. God uses all things for His Glory and your benefit. **Romans 8:28** says, **"And we know that in all things God works for the good of those who love him, who have been called according to his purpose."**

I remember driving to work many times with the heavy metal music cranked up, singing like I just didn't

Jeff Lacki

care, and I didn't. I'd just assume beat someone up as be nice to them if they looked at me funny. Satan had really gripped my heart and turned me against God. From that point on, I would talk to women online and see if they lived near me, find out if they were cute or not, and see what would come of it. The good part of all of this was that I was always a very picky person when it came to women. San Jose had a low percentage of women to men as well, so meeting someone at work or in day to day life was not happening for me.

I met a bunch of women who lived on the West Coast and specifically California over a several month period of time. One girl from Seattle, Washington started chatting with me, and we seemed to become pretty close very quickly. We started talking on the phone and swapped photos. For whatever reason, she told me she loved me and really cared about me. She decided to come visit me in California for the weekend. When she arrived things were great, but shortly after that she started getting cold towards me. I won't get into all the details of our couple days together, but this was the first time I really cared about someone and they broke my heart. She had told me all these things before she met me and then when she came, she did a complete 180. I never did know why, but my point is that she really broke my heart, brief as our "relationship" had been.

This small heartache furthered the wound that Satan had been digging in my heart against God, what little of God was even left at that point. I remember crying over this because I was so hurt, and I have never been one to cry too much, ever.

Shortly after that, I met a girl who was 19 who went to school in Santa Barbara. We started chatting and flirting online for a few weeks. One day, I started feeling lumps in my neck and went to the doctor's office. He sent me for a blood test and found out I had mononucleosis. I had been burning the candle at both ends and getting very little sleep. I would stay up late chatting online, go to work, and then come home and train in martial arts. It got so bad that I started taking Nyquil to help me fall asleep. I had also broken my knee playing indoor soccer about 2 months prior and was taking up to 8 Advil at a time for the swelling and pain.

The day I found out I had mono officially, I had talked to her and told her I was sick. She offered to take care of me. I decided to drive down there for several days and take her up on her offer, which, looking back was odd because I had never seen what she looked like. From that point on we had a "relationship." I should also mention that I had been talking to a psychic woman who was a friend of a friend of mine. She had told me that at some point I was going to have to decide between two women. This was before I knew or dated anyone, so I laughed and told her that will be the day! I also told her that would be a good thing in my miserable life, the day I would have a choice of women.

It's interesting to me how Satan somehow, sometimes knows the future, at least in part. Psychics do possess real power, but it is not of the Lord. It is demonic power. The things this woman told me were right about 50% of the time, so I believed her enough to keep going back to her. I should mention also that I had for years believed in UFOs, ghosts, and the paranormal. It all fascinated me. Even as a Catholic, I believed that reincarnation was real and that maybe I really did have past lives, although I couldn't quite reconcile reincarnation with the what the Bible taught about death. I also had some type of aversion to the desert southwest. I don't know why, but somehow I felt that if I really did have a past life or two, I had lived there as well. I can see now that that was probably God's impression on my own heart for future events since I just moved to Phoenix and am awaiting Gods next assignment for my life. Deuteronomy 18 clearly speaks against such things as divination, sorcery, interpreting omens, casting spells, witchcraft, mediums and spiritists. If I knew that the Bible was real and had read it, I would have known better, but I didn't yet.

After I was born again and the Lord began to teach me and open my eyes to the truth, I realized how stupid and silly that belief was and is, as well as reincarnation, UFOs and ghosts. Ghosts are nothing more than demons masquerading as humans who have died. Reincarnation doesn't exist of course; once we are dead, we are dead. **"Just as man is destined to die once, and after that to face judgment, so Christ was sacrificed once to take way the sins of many people; and he will appear a second time, not to bear sin, but to bring salvation to those who are waiting for him"** **(Hebrews 9:27–28).** As a Catholic I had also believed in "purgatory." I now realized that there was no such thing or place as "purgatory." It was and is yet another demonic teaching to mislead people so they will parish eternally on the day of their natural death. Once you are dead, you are dead. That's why Jesus Christ died, so we wouldn't have to face eternal condemnation and go to Hell if we are in Him. If there was such a place as "purgatory," there would be no reason for Jesus to die for our sins; His death would have been for naught. We would just be able to work out our own salvation in purgatory. I won't even get into UFOs as my beliefs may not line up with yours; however, I do know that Jesus Christ is alive and well without a shadow of a doubt. I do not believe that Jesus went to other planets and died for alien races to save them; nor do I believe that there is any life whatsoever in the entire universe other than on planet Earth–intelligent life anyhow. God created everything just for us because of his great love for us. **"For God so loved the world that He gave his one and only Son, that whoever believes in him shall not perish but have eternal life" (John 3:16).** Somehow Satan and his kingdom are involved in all of these diversions that go on in this world that lead people away from the truth. **Hosea 4:6** says: **"...my people are destroyed from lack of knowledge."** God is saying that HIS people are destroyed, not people who are unsaved, who are already perishing due to their unbelief. This scripture does not mean they perish in Hell. They have already accepted Jesus and believe in Him. It refers to being destroyed here on Earth because they don't understand the more meaty things of the Bible, which keep them in bondage to the lies and deceptions of the enemy.

This is a word the Lord spoke to us one evening at a prayer meeting about the stars, the universe, and His death on the Cross:

My children, it was in passion that I stretched forth my hand and I spoke that the stars would hang in the heavens.

And it was in love that I spoke and I stretched forth my hand and the Earth appeared with all of its life and all of its beauty.

And it was in all of my passion and all of my

love, with these same hands, that I stretched them forth and I was lifted to the Cross, that they would be pierced, and that I would bear the weight of the world on my shoulders - upon Me!

The hands that formed the Earth, yet they were crushed with the weight of sin.

It is these same hands, my children, these same hands, that I extend to you now and I say to you,

"Come to Me, my children. Come to Me that I would place my hands upon you."

And in passion and in love I would speak to you and I would cleanse you and I would mold you into the people that I desire you to be; that you would be my warrior, that you would be my children, that you would be a light unto this world, and that I would use you for the days ahead.

For even on the Cross, did I not fulfill what was written?

Was not every word lifted up and fulfilled in Me?

And so it is my children, there are other words that have been written, there are other words that are yet to be fulfilled.

Let my hand be upon you and I will use you, my children.

My Word will be fulfilled in your lives.

You will go forth in power.

You will go forth in faith.

And you will be used by my Spirit.

For this is as it has been written, this is as I desire, this is how it shall be, my children.

I will make it so.

You will be my weapons.

You will be used by Me.

For I have declared it my children; it is written long ago - of ancient days, it is written, and so it shall be, my children.

My hands, my children.

My own hands.

My own hands formed this world.

My own hands saved this world.

My own hands, my children - upon your lives!

Upon your hearts!

My hands, my children.

My hands for you.

That summer I met another girl online who went to school in Southern California. I was what was called a channel operator of a room on IRC (internet relay chat) system. It had become a place where I was popular. My quick whit and humor also played a part because as operator, you could kick people out of the room with a message saying why they were being booted. One night in particular, when my future girlfriend came into the room, all of the girls were paying attention to me because I was booting what I termed as "lamers" left and right for being stupid. She started to as well. I can't remember what she said, but all I remember was kicking her out with a message saying "Come back when you know what you really want." It was almost prophetic for why we broke up 3 years later. She never seemed to make decisions well and was pulled and pushed by other people a lot in life by what they thought rather than her own strength.

That was how I met her. We talked more and became friends online. Then it moved to phone conversations quickly, and very shortly she was coming home to live for the summer with her parents near me. We met and became friends. After a week or so, she found out that the other 19 year old girl from Santa Barbara was coming to spend the night with me in my apartment. She already knew about the other 19 year old in my life. She gave me an ultimatum: If the 19 year old came to stay with me, don't call back. The decision of two women came to pass just as the psychic had told me. The interesting thing was, I wanted to date the new girl and dump the old one. The new one seemed very special, yet she was unwilling to give me any kind of commitment that she would date me exclusively. This was also another prophetic sign of things to come that ended our relationship later. I ended up dumping the 19 year old girl for the 21 year old girl the next day.

We started dating all that summer and made it official to be boyfriend and girlfriend just before she went back to college in Southern California. We also started having sex that summer. It's interesting to note that I had met another cute girl across the way from my apartment who was a born again Christian just before all of this started. We were just friends. She told me that sex was special and she was waiting until she got married. I was impressed, but told her I was 28 and didn't plan on waiting any longer. "God" hadn't answered my most basic prayer of even having a girlfriend, let alone sex, since I was 6. I wasn't about to wait any longer. If I found someone willing, I was going to do it. After all, God wasn't answering my prayers, and I really didn't care or much believe in Him any longer. I was still far too hurt to care what God thought, especially since His "love" for me was causing me so much pain and heartache.

When my new girlfriend and I started dating, she was the sweetest, nicest, and seemingly most mature girl I had ever met for being 21 years old. She was, from my standpoint, pure and honest, loving, loyal and kind. She was a Greek Orthodox Catholic, so our belief systems were very similar. Her parents were more Christian than Catholic. To this day, I believe God sent her into my life so that my heart would not become cold and hard towards Him any further. She really did show me the good in life and brought back my faith in God without even knowing it. Little did I know that that relationship was going to be my most wonderful experience, as well as the most painful time in my entire life.

Jeff Lacki

How Did I Get Here?

I remember the days of "Egypt" in my life–that is, before I was "born again" and trusted in the Lord. They seem so long ago, and yet so recent all at once. My life now is focused on the Lord, and the things of Heaven and His Kingdom, and His purposes for my life. I've been unemployed now for over 4 years from software engineering. It wasn't always like this. I was once a brand new baby in the Lord. I didn't know the difference between Saul and Paul, let alone who Paul was in the Bible. I knew there were 4 gospels, Revelation, and Genesis, and possibly a few other books if you pressed me. But the Bible was a bit foreign to me back then even though I had grown up in Catechism and the Catholic church. I don't ever recall hearing the Salvation message in Catechism or the Catholic Church, at least not as a pointed topic. They probably skimmed over it and danced around it, but nobody ever taught it to me point blank that I must be born again to go to heaven and be "saved."

I had started reading the Bible more seriously about 3 years before I officially gave my life to Jesus. My best friend at the time, Jason, was murdered in December 1995. I remember that date because I had called him a couple hours before it happened. I had asked him if he and his girlfriend wanted to go to Lake Tahoe with me and my girlfriend for New Year's Eve, and stay at a cabin that a bunch of co-workers rented. That evening I left with my girlfriend to go to her house (which was on the way to Tahoe). From there we would go up to Tahoe for a couple days. By the time I returned, spent another night at her place, then went back to work and then got home, about 5 days had passed. I had about 10 calls on my answering machine from various friends asking me to call them, and a couple of them telling me a bit about what happened. Jason's next door neighbor in the duplex was separated from her husband. Her estranged husband decided to go there and apparently murder his wife. She had 3 friends with her that evening and apparently all 3 were stabbed but not critically. Jason's throat was cut. They found him a minute or two before he died laying in the yard, bleeding to death and unconscious. He died before they could help him. The man who killed my friend is now in jail for at least 30 years until he can possibly get out for parole, last I heard.

Needless to say, this was a shock to me. I was in disbelief for several days. Jason was my closest friend. He was also one of my Tae Kwon Do instructors. We had all gone on a rafting and camping trip the summer before. We would hang out together outside the studio. I don't remember crying so much in all my previous years as I did then. I stayed home from work for 4 days and just cried on and off. But the Holy Spirit was working on me. It caused me to ask an age-old question: "Why do bad things happen to good people?" I was raised a Catholic. When I went to college, going to church was no longer a part of my life. My parents had forced me to go when I was at home. I remember asking my mom one Sunday when I was 16 what the purpose of going to church was really for. All we did was stand, sit, kneel, and repetitively say some belief doctrines of the Catholic Church over and over. Yes, there were a few minutes where a small reading from the Gospels was read, and then the Homily, which as far as I was concerned was the most interesting part of the whole time at church. The music, to my ears, was dry and un-interesting, which further made me think that God didn't care too much about things in life. As long as we were basically "good," I'd see Him when I died. There was the Eucharist as well. No one had ever said anything about not partaking of the body of Christ (The Eucharist) if you didn't believe in Christ to begin with, since **1 Corinthians 13:29–30** says, **"For anyone who eats and drinks without recognizing the body of the Lord eats and drinks judgment on himself. That is why many among you are weak and sick, and a number of you have fallen asleep."** So we put our hour in at church and that's all God cared about, so I thought. I couldn't say for sure if I was going to get into Heaven, but hoped I would be going there, seeing as how I was mostly "good" and "moral." How deceived I already was without knowing it, and there was nobody so far who told me the truth!

With my friend dead, I started reading the Bible a little bit. It was not much–maybe a chapter a month–which back then seemed like a lot. I didn't start reading because I thought that I would find answers to my questions. I started reading because I wondered what the Bible actually had in it beyond what I had heard over the years. I didn't seek after God. I went on with my life, putting the past behind me as best as I could, and writing it off as "life happens." Almost one year later, another friend of Jason and mine committed suicide after his fiancé had broken up with him. He hung himself in the garage. His fiancé found him there. Our friend Joe had suffered with clinical depression apparently for years, we later found out. I had really had a great friendship with Joe until the year before when he met this girl. Joe drifted away from all of us. Nevertheless, his sudden death and its circumstances both shocked me and also opened up the previous years wound and question: "Why do bad things happen to good people?" Once again I was asking God what was going on. Looking back, things seem much clearer for what God was doing in my life. I have no idea what it was doing in others' lives at that time, but both deaths affected me greatly; yet life still had to go on without them. I had lost many relatives as a young teenager–my grandfather, uncle, aunt, great grandfather and great grandmother all from the age of 8 through 13–but this was different. Still I continued to read the Bible on and off. God was working. **"For my thoughts are not your thoughts, neither are your ways my ways, declares the Lord. As the heavens are higher than the earth, so are my ways higher than your ways and my thoughts than your thoughts." (Isaiah 55:8–9).** I do believe that when we die, God will show us every reason for the bad things that happened to us. God does not waste bad things in our lives "just because." God has a purpose for all things, great or small.

One night, the Lord spoke to us about this very verse as we had been discussing it amongst ourselves:

My children, you have said the words this evening that your ways are not my ways - it is true, my children!

It is right that you would say this, for truly you would see this world, you would look upon my creation, and you would know that it is beyond you, it is beyond your ways - for this world is my way, my children.

But even so, I tell you that my ways are your ways, for my ways are for you, my children.

My way is truth - it is truth for you, my children.

My way is holiness - and you must be holy, my children.

My way is the way of love - it is love for you, my children; love must be your way.

My ways are your ways, my children, and that is what this life is about, that in my creation, in this world, that you would learn my ways and you would grow in Me.

This is my desire, my children, that my ways would become as your ways because of the love that you would have for Me, because of the desire that you would have for Me, because of the willingness you would have, my children, even as the willingness that I showed you that I went to the Cross for you and I died to self.

So it is for you, my children, that you must die to self, that you would desire my ways and not your own, my love and not your own, my holiness and not your own, my truth, my children, before the truth of this world.

Before the truth of your own mind, it must be my truth, and it is in prayer, my children, and reading of the Word that you would come upon these things and that I would strengthen you and that I would make you as a new person; you would be reborn, my children!

Others would look upon you and they would not recognize you because it is my way upon you, my children.

It is my way for all things.

It is my way I make for you.

It is my way that I pave the path and I call you upon.

Come this way, my children.

Come to Me.

I have prepared the way.

I have spoken of the way.

It is the way for you, my children.

I am the way.

I am the way.

Come to Me, my children.

I am the way.

Moving forward another year or so, my girlfriend and I were starting to have more serious problems in our relationship. The same girlfriend that had been with me through both friends' deaths started changing in front of my eyes. Her ex-boyfriend had been sending her love letters for about a year on and off. She finally told me this just after her college graduation, 2 years after we started dating. She was struggling over him and wondering about things with him. I listened and tried to support her through her confusion over this past guy, but never thought it would lead to a serious problem in our relationship. Nor could I understand any of the confusion to begin with. To me it was clear; I treated her great, loved her deeply, and yet some past relationship was bothering her. It just didn't add up. She kept telling me how I was the best thing that ever happened to her. She didn't know why she felt this way about this guy who was so obviously not right for her. This guy had been her first sexual experience. I later read a book long after I was saved called **"Seductions Exposed"** by Dr Gary L. Greenwald about, among other things, women and their first sexual encounters and the spiritual implications of sex. This book gave me the answers I had been looking for of why she did what she did. This happened in October 1997, just before the summer I got saved in 1998. She briefly met him secretly, and I later found out. I speak more about this shortly.

It's amazing how much clarity I have now over those events, both in the natural and the spiritual. But at the time, it was yet another wrench in the life that I was trying to make work and make conform to what I wanted my life to be. The Lord later spoke this word to me concerning that very issue:

My son, you would stand before the field and you would look upon it, and great would be your sorrow, great would be your despair, for you know this field well.

With your own hands you have tilled it.

With your own hands you have planted.

With your own hands you have watered, and you would look upon it in its devastation, for where is the crop that you have planted?

What has it yielded you in your life?

For the rains have not come and the field did not grow and there is no harvest for you, and all your hopes were upon the field, your very life was in the field.

I tell you the truth my son, that in your life you have been as a beautiful vase, fragile.

If one would touch it wrong it would shatter.

If it gets banged, it is destroyed.

If it is dropped, it is no more.

You are as a vase that must be kept on a shelf,

and then people will look upon it, they will see the beauty and they will cherish it.

The glory of the vase will shine.

My son, it is my will that you would not be as the vase, that instead, I would use you.

Instead, I would call you to a field that I have planted, that I have planted the seed, that I have tilled the soil, that I have made ready for what will become the Harvest.

It is not the fragile vase that would reap the Harvest, it is a working vase.

It is a vase that is strong.

It is a vase to be used by the hands of the Harvester and taken to the field and placed in the dirt and filled with the harvest.

My son, is this not the time of your testing?

Is this not the time that I would toughen you?

That I would take a glass that is thin and beautiful and I would make it thick and strong?

In this time my son, it is my desire that you would become strong, that you would see the testing that is upon you, and in it all, you would say "Blessed be the name of the Lord."

That you would see the trial that is upon you and in it all, your heart would be for Me.

For this is my Glory my son, it is my joy and it is your life, that you would be used by Me; that you would take this test and you would pass it my son, and surely you will pass it.

Surely my hand will be upon you and I will strengthen you.

Surely I will take you upon the hill and you will

not look behind you at the field that is destroyed, the field of your dreams that have not come true.

You will look upon the field of my planting.

The field of beauty, the field of glory, and you will be ready for the tasks that I have given you, that in faith, in strength, in perseverance, in character, in love, you will do the work of my hand, for I will have prepared it for you my son.

You will look back upon this time, it will be a witness to others, even as it will witness to you, even as you will know that I have been God, even in your time of despair.

It is the field that you would look upon my son, you make the choice, you make the choice my son.

Is it the field that you would plant or is it the field that I have created?

I believe that God was starting to break us apart. I should clarify—God was allowing events to unfold that were putting his plans and purposes for our lives into action. Her life, for some direction which I may never know; and my life, for the calling that God placed upon me before the foundation of the world. I, obviously, was clueless. All I knew was I was again in great pain. Even as Job didn't understand his great calamities in the Bible, so much more did I not understand anything that was going on in my life. I felt so lost and confused most every day. All I knew was that I was entering into the most painful part of my entire life...and the most beautiful in God's eyes.

We both ended up breaking up just 3 months before the wedding. Actually, I broke it off with her. She wasn't able to make any real decisions in her life, including in our relationship. So I walked away from the one and only woman I had ever loved up to that point in my life.

As I touched upon earlier, her ex-boyfriend had met her secretly about 8 months earlier at a conference she attended in Palm Springs for the doctors' office she worked for. He lived thirty minutes away from Palm Springs, and she decided not to tell me that he was going to come up and see her while she was there. After that I basically said, we've been dating for a while and its time to get engaged or break up. I put no real pressure on her to get engaged, but I did lay out how I was feeling about our relationship. She decided that I was the one she wanted, and we were engaged Christmas of 1997. A couple months after our engagement, we went to Cancun together, our first real vacation. There was already something cold about her after we arrived in Cancun but I couldn't put my finger on it. We had our differences at times, but it was beyond that this time. It was during a walk back from one of the clubs we went to one evening that I felt the strangest thing. I felt as though I didn't know her any longer, as if I was walking next to someone I had just met for the first time. It was after this trip that things went downhill very quickly. I believe that was the defining moment in the spirit where God removed his will that we stayed together any longer. Upon our return, I started getting accused of all sorts of things–inabilities to do this or that. Some were true, most were not. She accused me of changing now that I "had" her and we were engaged. The truth was, she was getting cold feet and was putting the blame on me. That, and the fact that she allowed everyone else's opinion to affect her own. It was in the weeks that followed that we had to send invites to the wedding out to our families who lived in both Los Angeles and Chicago. After a couple weeks of indecision on her part, her father and I decided to call off the wedding since she had serious cold feet and couldn't make the decision to move forward with the wedding to save her life. I was pretty disgusted with her inabilities at this point and her accusations against me.

About 6 weeks later, a few of her out of town friends came to town and they went out dancing. I later found out she met a guy there and her friends encouraged her to call him and go out with him afterwards. So she did, without telling me. I should add we were still engaged at this point. She saw him a couple or few times within a 2 week period. Unfortunately I didn't find this information out until I was already driving down to Arizona two weeks later with her. She had applied to medical school to be a PA (Physicians Assistant) and had gotten in at the very last minute on the alternate list. I had decided to go to Arizona for 2 reasons. One, that I was still her boyfriend/fiancé. Secondly, I had originally wanted to move to Phoenix anyhow. The truth came out when we stopped to get lunch. We were driving separately. I asked her about something she said to one of these girlfriends on the phone the night before, which didn't sit right with me. She had said, "No, not yet," as if her girlfriend had asked her about something that she couldn't answer freely in front of me. It was a red flag.

She had applied to medical school that last October when our first troubles started. At the last minute she was accepted on the alternate list. Looking back, I wish I had turned around and went back home immediately to leave her to her life right there and then. I should have, but I wasn't strong enough to do it at that time. I had to endure her allowing this guy to call her at my cousin's house. We were both staying there until we each could get an apartment or house. When I confronted her on this, she told me it was my job to tell him not to call anymore. I bluntly told her, "No, it is *your* job," especially if she actually cared about me, which she didn't anymore. She was just afraid of doing it herself, I think.

God was working again, this time to separate me for a much better life (ultimately) and his calling upon my life. I had moved to Arizona with her as she entered medical school at the last minute. I had found a job within 1 week at a company where a charismatic Catholic named Ron was working. I told him on the first day that my world had just fallen apart, and He started to share Christ with me. He and I worked together. During this time, he shared Christ with me in a way I had never known Jesus before. It was personal, it was real, and it was powerful! His testimonies of miracles and things the Lord had done kept me in awe listening to them, one after another. Now this was a true God, I thought to myself! Not the "go to church every week and nothing happens, same old same old God who almost never shows himself to us." After only 4 weeks in Arizona, I gave my girlfriend an ultimatum. Either we moved into an apt together and she re-dedicated herself to me, and I became her boyfriend again (I had told her on the way down when I found out about the other guy she was no longer my girlfriend by her own actions), or I was leaving her for good–end of story. I had put up with her emotional torture and abuse long enough. I had been the best boyfriend she said she ever had, yet her actions were contrary to what she said. And I tried my best to treat her as best as I could, even in the midst of being abused by her. She said no, so from that point

Jeff Lacki

on, I gave my two week notice and started looking for work back in California. She really didn't believe I was going to leave her, she later told me. The morning I left for home, I felt the happiest I had been during that whole miserable 2–3 month period. I left to return back to California where, on the very first weekend arriving home, I started back at the Assembly of God church where my former girlfriend and I had started going on and off 8 months earlier. I don't recall them ever giving the call for salvation until that morning when I raised my hand and gave my heart to the Lord. There was nothing special about it, to me at least. I was just in intense pain. That's when everything changed, and I didn't even know it yet. I was in so much emotional pain and confusion; I knew that I couldn't live any longer without God in my life. It was the God that my friend Ron had shared with me in Arizona. I needed *that* God. I needed Jesus Christ.

I certainly had no control over my life. Then again, I *never* really did. I only *thought* I did, like most people.

Many people who don't know the Lord talk about how Christians are weak minded, unintelligent, etc. What they don't understand is that when God allows circumstances in your life, whoever you are, you too will become weak, confused, and desperate for something more than yourself. **"He who falls on this stone will be broken to pieces, but he on whom it falls will be crushed" (Matthew 21:44).** It's only in situations where you are helpless that you, as an unbeliever, generally cry out to God for help. The Lord told me that if He had put an average person through some of the things that He put me through, they would have been finished. I presume He meant dead, but He is and has been training me for greater things and use for His Kingdom–and if you are reading this book, very possibly you as well! Jesus said, **"Take my yoke upon you and learn from me, for I am gentle and humble in heart, and you will find rest for your souls" (Matthew 11:29)**. The world says be bold, confident, outgoing, and to grab all the gusto you can get your hands on. Satan is the ruler of this world, at the moment. God is only allowing him to remain in control for a short while longer.

The Lord told me over a year later how he started to pull things together for me when I gave my heart to Him that morning at church.

My son, you would stand with your feet in the sand and you would look to the ocean and you would see the water before you; it would extend greatly into the ocean, it would be vast before your eyes, and it is more than you can see.

And as far as you can see, the water is peaceful, the water is calm.

My son, the wave breaks close to the beach.

I tell you the truth, that the wave would start miles from the shore, far beyond your vision, yet it would gain momentum and it would come to the shore and you would not see it - the surface would be peaceful.

It gathers momentum and speed and as it rushes to the earth, it is then that the wave would lift, it is then that you would see it, it is then you would recognize the power and the force of the wave though moments before you did not see it.

Let this be your encouragement my son.

Let this be your life.

That all things are in motion, that all things have begun for you.

Since you accepted Me in your heart, at that time, my son, I began to pull things together for you.

And the wave is building in your life; though you would look to the ocean now and your heart would desire to see the wave, you would desire to know it and to see it coming.

Yet you do not - yet be encouraged, my son, for the wave breaks late!

The wave breaks as the water rushes to the shore.

And so it shall be in your life.

Do not give up hope!

Do not be discouraged!

Do not stop looking for the wave!

For surely it is coming, my son.

These are my words to you:

Seek Me, my son.

Let your eyes be upon Me.

Let your heart be filled with joy.

For all things in your life I have brought about and I am working in your life.

My son, learn what you would in these times.

Desire Me, that is what I say.

Desire Me!

For just as the wave would come close to the shore, so it shall be for you, and you will see the wave break and it will be beautiful to you, my son.

It will be filled with power and strength.

This is my desire, my son - so it shall be.

So it shall be for you.

For the next full year, I attended church weekly, read my Bible more and prayed.

The ex-girlfriend kept calling me and playing the emotional games with me, as if we were still dating. I admit, I wanted to tell her to take a hike permanently, but I was still too weak to do so. After all, I really did love her. I believe I loved her far more than she ever loved me, but I don't know. Finally in late October 1998, I told her don't ever call me again. She was coming home for Thanksgiving and Christmas breaks, but I didn't care. I was sick of being used like an old rag doll for her entertainment when she felt like she needed me.

After only 2 or 3 weeks, I got a phone call at work just a couple days before she was coming home. She was crying on the other end, telling me how much her heart hurt and how much she missed me. I felt bad for her. I still loved her. I tried to remain strong and say "too bad," but I was still weak. I told her I would see her when she came home.

During Thanksgiving and Christmas, I told her how badly she had treated me and I didn't deserve it. It was wrong, and supposedly I was the best thing that had happened to her. I told her she had a bad way of showing me. We reconciled, and I told her that either we got married shortly or it was over completely. I wasn't messing around anymore. I had already been through the hardest part of the breakup. I said, we either get married before she returns to school or it's over. In her classic style of duck and delay, she told me she needed to figure out her schedule when she returned to school and she would let me know shortly. After 2 weeks went by, my mother got on my case over the whole thing. It is true; love is blind. I was so blind. I was smack me on the head, stupid blind, honestly. But my mom was right. She was just playing her usual emotional games with me. I hung up the phone with my mom and then called her and told her it was over, and not to ever call me back again. After the usual tears and words from her, I hung up.

Not 3 days went by and I received a call from her. I had told her long before this that I only ask someone to marry me once in their lifetime; never again would I ask her to marry me. She knew this and so she asked me to marry her over the phone. I reiterated that I wasn't waiting. She had 2 weeks to marry me and then I was walking. Was I dumb or what? At this point most of you, including myself looking back, are probably wondering why I was so stupid. I really was. But as I said, love makes you do dumb things and make bad choices sometimes, especially if you aren't strong. This happened on a Sunday. I accepted her proposal By Wednesday, when I spoke to her, I started to hear the same old confusion in her voice. I questioned her about it, and she told me that she had to get used to things again or something like that. This was getting quite old by now, so once again, I said it's over. It is completely over. I don't want to marry you. I don't want to date you. I would have to live in the same town as you to ever even consider dating you, and even then it wouldn't happen. It wasn't until this time that she finally realized how over it really was. She started to experience the same pain I had been experiencing for months. Apparently she had been in denial since the summer. I have no idea. She was crying once again and honestly, I just didn't care anymore. She was a quite attractive woman. Even my friends asked me how I was with her, presuming I was not as good looking as she was. That didn't matter to me anymore. She may have been beautiful, but her inside was not. It had turned quite ugly. There were many other minor details, but I don't think it would benefit you, the reader, to add any more. I also don't want this to appear as bashing her or getting even. The truth is, it's been 7 yrs and I'm well over her. I praise the Lord He has healed the wounds related to that time. I still have scars, however, and one typically never forgets the pain they went through when someone has hurt them badly. Honestly, I feel sorry for her now, especially if she doesn't know Christ yet. She finally honored my request and I haven't spoken to her in over 6 years now. The experience made me far stronger than I ever thought possible, which was part of God's purpose.

I was still reeling in the pain and devastation and loss over my former relationship during all this time. I spent many weekends on my knees crying before God in complete isolation and loneliness. I knew she was out and about meeting guys and would have a boyfriend in no time. At that time it bothered me a lot, obviously, but I also knew I didn't want her back, ever. I had even told the Lord that I didn't want Him to bring her back to me. I wanted someone new, even though I realized He can restore all things if He wants to. I don't think I ever cried so much in my entire life as I did during those months. This time, I cried far more than when my friends had died–far, far more. The pain wasn't all due to my relationship. It was everything–everything that had gone wrong in my life, everything that I had worked so hard to attain and yet not attained it. Yes, the heartache over love lost was the most significant, but looking back, that wasn't the whole story. God indeed humbled me. God indeed was working in a way in which I had never known God would work. But then again, I didn't truly know God before. I was only now starting to learn the Bible and who God truly was—His character, His ways, how He deals with his children, and how He deals with sinners. I spent that entire year alone for the most part. I had no friends, my family was all back east, and I had yet to know anyone at church yet or get involved. I went to church every Sunday and came home. I had a couple relatives in the area, but like work relationships, they can't empathize with your pain as much as your close family or friends would. So I rarely talked about the intense pain I was going through. In fact, I used to take two 15 minute breaks a day and go for a walk alone, praying and talking to God. I remember asking, even praying for Him to kill me on a daily basis, literally. I could hardly stand to be in my own body, it hurt so much. I knew Heaven was real. I knew Jesus was real. Heaven was so awesome and my pain so deep, all I wanted to do was go to Heaven and be with Him. I knew suicide was out of the question; besides, I would never want to hurt anyone here on Earth after my death that way. So I struggled on one day at a time, feeling as though those days would never ever end. They seemed endless! I was so humbled. I remember driving to work everyday. The attitude I once had about people cutting me off or riding my bumper didn't phase me a bit. I just didn't care. Those things were not important, and if they wanted to do that, it was fine by me. I thought to myself one day how different I had become through this experience, but also, how good it was that I didn't hold anger towards other drivers as I had before. I started to feel sorry for those types of people. They were speeding around in their life and yet really, spiritually, not going anywhere. It really put my life in focus to the things that really mattered most.

At another prayer meeting, the Lord spoke this word concerning trials in life and the clarity it brings:

My children, these are my words my children, that it is in the coldness of the night, it is in the coldest of nights that the most amazing things would appear in the skies, that you would look and there would be clarity and you would see millions of stars, more than you would have thought existed.

It is in the coldness of the night my children that there is clarity, and for you it is in the trial of your life that you would look for Me and you would seek Me, and it is in those times that you will see Me, with greater clarity, even as the stars would fill the sky and many times you would not look for them, and even as you would look you would not see, yet as you search for Me in your trial, as you look for Me, when the circumstances are difficult, it is then that you will see, there is more of Me than you had known.

There is more of Me than you have seen, and the clarity will come upon you, and you will know, and you will never forget my children.

Even in times when your vision is not as clear, even in times where you will not see, yet you will remember, yet you will know that night that you stood and you looked at the stars and you saw so much and it seemed so close, always there is more, always I am close my children and you will remember those times, even if you were not living them in the moment you will know because they are part of your life, even as I am a part of your life.

Look to the stars in the coldness my children.

Look to Me in your trial, for you shall find Me and you shall see Me.

Your lives will not be the same my children.

There is a reason for the trial.

Search for it my children.

Search for it and you will find it, and when you find it, will it not be my own hands that will hold you?

Will it not be my own arms that you will fall within?

It is always Me my children, it is always Me.

At the end of that year, the Lord had been speaking to my heart over and over in church service about cell groups that met every week. I was playing soccer 3 times a week at the time, as well as training for my black belt in Tae Kwon Do, which was getting closer and closer. It was my only true joy in midst of my pain, and I didn't want to let them go. But I decided that if **"God is a rewarder of those who diligently seek Him" (Hebrews 11:6),** then I could sacrifice 1 game a week and attend a meeting for Him. I made a call to the church and got 2 phone numbers. One meeting met on Wednesday and the other on Tuesday. I decided that the Tuesday night meeting was good because I didn't have to give up soccer on Wednesday night. I also realized in my little faith, that if God intended for me to go, Tuesday night must be the one He wanted since that's what I was choosing to do. It turned out I was right. God led me to the greatest group of people I had ever met. Even to this day they are as close as my natural family.

The Lord is Real!

It was during these prayer meetings that the Lord was using my friends to speak to me prophetically, as I have included already throughout the book. God was speaking to me through my friend, sharing His heart about me and my life, and even my future in Him and for Him. Sometimes the Lord would tell me things at the meeting that I had been praying or asking about that past week or sometimes even that same day. My friend with the prophetic gift had no idea that I had been praying about these things, and yet the Lord used him to speak to me about those very same things. It was amazing! My faith was growing to a new level. God was becoming more and more real each week I met with Him at the meetings!

It was during these prayer meetings that the Lord was starting to reveal Himself to me. It was not just prophetically, but also to my spiritual sensitivity of His Spirit moving in the room. Over the course of time, I had begun to put two and two together. I realized that whenever I felt (physically) this particular sensation on my head, the Holy Spirit was present. The moment that this reality truly struck me most was at a particular prayer meeting in which a friend of ours, Pastor Varkey Varghese from Light of Life Church in New York City, had come and was praying for people.

I had met Pastor Varkey a couple months prior at my friends' house where we held our weekly prayer meetings. Pastor is an Indian man, originally from India. I have to tell this story because of the humor and blessing of this man and his family in my life. Where we lived in San Jose, there were lots of Indian people due to the high tech industry. I have always been a bit of a comic, and I had often impersonated Indian people with my friends and family–just for fun, not to be cruel or mean. The fact is, I enjoy impersonating a lot of different people. I often watch how people act or respond, almost studying people in general as well–why they do what they do, etc. On that particular night, I walked in and saw Pastor sitting on the couch. I didn't know what to say. I also didn't realize the type of man he was in the Lord. By the end of the night, I found out just what a powerful man of God he is. Before I was about to leave, he asked me for my name, address and phone number to stay in touch with me. I have always been leery of giving my personal information out to anyone. Since I didn't really know him, I felt funny giving it to him. After all, he may actually call me and I could barely understand his English. Looking back, it seems quite funny. We often joke about it all, but at the time I was not so open to it. However, I did give him my information.

I tell that story to testify to the things that God sometimes brings us. They are not always packaged in the way we think they ought to be as blessings, but in reality they are the biggest blessings, if we choose to accept them. Pastor and his family are just like my own family now. I travel to New York City several times a year to visit and help with their church. I enjoy their fellowship, as well as the Lord's presence, each time we are together. I'm so happy I didn't say no to the Spirit concerning this man. Before my first trip to New York to visit Pastor, I was really reluctant to go. In all truth, I didn't ever want to go visit him. Not that I didn't enjoy

Jeff Lacki

him, but I was afraid of the unknown. Things like his family, what they may make for meals (I have always been a somewhat picky eater) made me reluctant. Silly things like that almost stopped me from receiving large blessings from our friendship by visiting New York. It was on my very first visit to Pastor's home that the Lord told me through Pastor that the Lord was giving me my future family. I was so young in the Lord; I expected it to happen within a month after I returned home! I laugh about that now, because as any mature believer knows, the Lord often gives you revelation sometimes years in advance of it actually happening. It nearly put a stumbling block before me because I was so upset by it not happening. Even now it is still unfulfilled, but I believe very, very soon in coming.

During Pastor Varkey's visit, we held several prayer meetings. As I was sitting in my chair at this particular prayer meeting, that same physical sensation started once again; however, this time it was very different than the other times. This time it felt more like a very large hand resting on my head, so much so that I had to put my own hand up there to see if someone was touching me. Of course, no one was. The anointing at that meeting was so heavy. It helped set me up for the next time it happened. The next amazing time that the Lord was revealing Himself to me was when a friend of mine and I went to southern California to a Christian conference. As we stood outside waiting for the doors to open for a couple hours, about 20 Christians who were in line started singing praise and worship songs to the Lord. I started singing as well and as I did, started to feel the presence of the Lord descend upon us. This time, the feeling I had was much more intense than the other experiences. The same physical sensation that was so strong lasted for an entire month before it ended. **John 14:21** says**, "Whoever has my commands and obeys them, he is the one who loves me. He who loves me will be loved by my Father, and I too will love him and show myself to Him."** God was continuing His promise in my life, continuing to lead me into deeper waters of His Spirit, and showing Himself to me in greater and greater ways. God *will* become more real to you as you obey Him and walk with Him. Satan gives out his power indiscriminately. God, however, will test you and try you before anointing you with real power from Heaven.

It was also during this time that the Lord led me to a Christian man I had been playing soccer with for months. A casual conversation after a soccer game turned into some things that led us both to realize that we were Christians. I started going to their Bible study meetings. It was then that the Lord led me to a new church, where I met more friends than I had ever had in my entire life. I add this to encourage anyone who is lonely for true friends from the Lord. The Bible says, **"But seek first his Kingdom and his righteousness, and all these things will be given to you as well" (Matthew 6:33)**. God knows your every need, even when you think He has forgotten you. I'm here to tell you, God never ever forgets about you. He knows the desires of your heart, and He shall fulfill them, in His time and in His way. It will always be better than you could have imagined it, or tried to make happen on your own! Another little "nugget" of wisdom about the Lord–there is always a time test. What I mean by this is there is always a period of time where God makes you wait, and it appears like nothing is happening or will happen. God did this to Joseph, who later became second in command of Egypt. He gave him a vision of his family bowing down to him, and allowed the direction of Joseph's life to go in the complete opposite direction for years before ending the test and bringing the vision to pass. The Lord may appear to "walk away" from us and find out if we are still hungry to follow after Him. Jesus did this after his resurrection to Cleopas and Simon in Luke 24:13–35. Jesus acted as if He was going to continue walking until the two urged Him to stay with them. No matter your thoughts, circumstances, or any situation you are in, continue to walk faithfully with the Lord.

Years of Hardship

As God often does in the Bible, I'm going back to the time I got saved to talk a bit more about the hardships these years have been. I'm not telling this story, or any other part of my life's story to dwell on my past. I thank God for what He allowed to come into my life, but at the time, it was the most painful experiences I have ever been through. The Lord has healed my heart and strengthened me more than I ever wanted to be strengthened. Many times the Lord spoke to me and told me how He knew I had wanted to turn from Him. In those same words to me, He told me He would never leave me or forsake me, even in those moments when I had temporarily turned my back on Him. I guess that's why He is God and I'm not. For as much as I considered myself a strong person, the events He brought into my life shook my life to its core. I've had no doubt there is a God and Jesus Christ is real–absolutely none. It has never been about believing if God exists during this last 7 years. It's been all about my own ability to withstand the pain of what God has been doing in my life through these various trials that have made me want to turn my back, even just for a moment, on the Lord.

My children, many times in my life I would hold the wood in my hand and I would see the shape and its form, yet I would put my hand to the task and I would take this wood and I would shape it and I would mold it - for I was known as the carpenter.

And so it was that I would work with the wood; I would make it into something useful or something beautiful, but I would take the raw form and I would change it.

And carefully I would chip away the parts that would not be used, the parts that would not bring beauty, until what I had formed in my mind was formed in the wood.

And so it is in your lives, my children, that even now I am still the carpenter and I would take you in my hand, I would take your lives and I would take your hearts, and I would see you in your raw form - and yet I would see ahead.

I would see you as perfection; I would see you in the image that I would shape with my own hand.

And I would chip away, my children.

I would shape you and I would mold you.

And this is the life that you live, and it is the life that I live with you.

For truly every day I am with you and I shape you and I mold you.

The day will come and you will be useful as there is need and you will be beautiful as there is need - for this is my desire.

This is my desire for you.

This is my desire for your lives.

After the breakup of my fiancé and I and giving my heart to the Lord, I honestly didn't want to live anymore. I was in so much pain, it was unbearable, literally. I couldn't stand to be in my own body at times. It's a feeling I cannot really explain, but if you have ever been in similar circumstances, you probably understand exactly what I mean.

I left Arizona, where I had briefly moved to be with my fiancé as she attended medical school, and returned to California where I hadn't sold my home yet, thank God! I spent several weeks looking for a software job again. After 1 month, I found one working at a well known medical company, doing software on blood analyzer equipment in a language called C++. Now up until this time I didn't really know C++, but I knew C, which is a predecessor to C++ and is used as part of the language as well. The reason I am going into this is that the job required an understanding of something I didn't know. It wasn't exactly easy to pickup and get hired for a job without some good experience. I remember my future boss telling me at the interview that he didn't care that I didn't know this language. He just wanted someone who had enough knowledge so he could teach them the language. Now it's interesting because I had wanted to learn this newer language for a while, but had found no one who would hire me because I had no experience in it whatsoever. The job gave me a $5,000 sign on bonus and a $7,000 yearly increase, as well and a promotion to senior software engineer and a very relaxed job atmosphere. Don't misunderstand me; the job was demanding, intellectually, but relaxed in the fact that the software schedule was not demanding. I look back on this time in amazement at how God took care of me. To be honest, I was hurting so badly I didn't care if I ever worked again, or lived for that matter. The slow pace of this job was definitely God's grace and mercy on me. I could barely focus on anything in my life, let alone what they were paying me to do. Somehow I did it. My co-workers were really great as well.

It was during this first job with the medical company I met the wonderful Christian brothers and sisters who mentored and discipled me in the small group meetings. The Lord began speaking to me immediately at the first meeting and started really encouraging me to keep the faith and walk with Him. This word is one of the first ones I received:

My son, you would stand on the shore of the lake and the water would stretch forth before you; you would see the reflections, my son - all that is glorious would be upon the water, for you would see the sky and the clouds as they would shine back to you from the water, you would see the glory of the mountain as it would reflect off the water.

And such is the time in your life, my son, that you would look on the water, you would see the glory and it would be your desire, but you would see as through a veil - it would not be clear, it would entice you, you would desire more, but you would not see the full glory.

Such is a time for you, my son, that I would ask you to turn; for the mountain stands tall behind you - tall and reaching to the sky, and I would ask that you would turn and look upon it that you would see it, not as a reflection, my son, not as one who would look away and yet seek to see, I ask that you would look into my eyes and into my face and that you would seek Me with all of your heart, my son, that you would seek Me with all that is within you, for so it is that you will find Me.

These things that you desire, the way that you desire to know Me, I am here, my son.

I am always with you.

Turn to Me.

Look upon Me.

You will see Me, my son, as you have not seen Me before.

Jeff Lacki

You will see Me, not as a reflection upon the water, but you will look upon the One who is real, the One who stands before you.

You will see the mountain, my son, you will know that it is Me.

You will know that I am in your life and that I am the Rock, my son, for you I do not change and I do not move.

I am in your life forever, my son - for all of time.

Know this in your heart, and continue in your ways, for as you do, my son, it is then you will see Me.

It is then you will see Me.

After about 1.5 yrs of working for the medical company, I went to another well known internet company for something more exciting and stock options. I was now giving my tithe to the Lord's work and wanted to give more, as well as make more of course. That job didn't work out and I went to 3 other jobs within about 1 year's time for various reasons. I started to wonder, why all the chaos? Before I was saved I had a nice stable job; things were going great. I made decent money at the time, and now that I know the Living God, my life seems all messed up. What's going on, God? I thought I was the son of the King, an heir of Heaven? The days of old seemed far better than this. I seem to remember a bunch of Israelites saying the same things over and over to the Lord in the desert for 40 years back in the Old Testament.

After the last job in that year's time, which I quit because the spiritual warfare between my boss and I was so bad I dreaded going into work anymore, the dot com bubble collapsed and nobody was hiring. I didn't think it would take too long to find a job, maybe a month or two, but certainly something would come up. That unemployment has now lasted over four years and counting, in which I sold every stock I had, my 401k, went through all my savings, you name it. The only things I had left were my possessions, including the house. The house is huge, don't misunderstand me. But you still need cash to live and pay bills. Other than that, I was poorer than I had ever been in my entire life with no end in sight. Sept 11, 2001 hit and I knew it was going to be a long haul. The so called "financial experts" kept saying how it was going to recover soon, but I knew it wasn't going to anytime soon. I didn't have to be a financial expert to see that!

As I prayed about leaving this last job, the Lord spoke this word to me, which encouraged me that my life is truly in His hands and not my own, no matter what happened:

My son, each day does not the sun break and come forth upon this Earth?

Each day my son if you would see this world from the height you would see how big it is, you would see it my son, that it is bigger than you would know; and I speak to you now as the geese of the air my son, from a great height.

They would look upon this earth and the sun would break forth they would see all the choices they would have.

Which way would they go?

Which way do they travel?

It all lays before them and the choice is theirs, or so it would seem my son.

It would seem as their own choice; and even as

it is their first flight; even as they have not made the trip before, is it not so for you my son?

That you are still young in Me, though you have grown, there is much more that you will learn, there is much more that you will know; and you are as on your first flight.

Which way to go?

I tell you my son that for the first time the geese would flee from the coming winter.

They would feel the changes upon them, they would know that it is time to fly.

They do not know where, and yet they rise, they rise in the air and I show them the way.

I guide them on my son, even as I guide you.

I show them the way, even as I show you; and I tell you, they do not become lost, even on the way, where they might lose track for a while, it is but for a while.

Still I lead them on, still I take them to their destination.

And so it shall be for you my son, that your destination is assured.

I know your path and I know where you will land my son.

I know the way for you.

Do not worry and do not shrink back for I have a plan for you.

And these are my words my son, these are my words for you:

That even as the goose does not fly alone, you should not fly alone either.

You should surround yourself with others.

Others who have made the trip before, others

who will show you the way, others who are strong in faith and strong in my Spirit.

These are my words for you, that you would fly as a flock my son, and others will help you and they will guide you along the way, and they will strengthen you; and as this happens my son you will see, the time will come and you yourself will be experienced, you yourself will mature and grow and it is then that I will bring others to you who are new, who have not flown before, and you will show them the way.

I will show you and you will show them.

This is my way for you my son.

I will use you, do not worry about that.

I will use you as you grow, as you learn I will use you more.

Remember my son, remember, the Earth stands before you and you have many choices to make but I will guide you, I will show you the way.

Do not worry my son, do not worry.

About 3 months after I quit this last job, I went on my first mission trip to Mexico to build small houses for poor people through the church I was attending in California. Interestingly enough, before I was saved, I had no desire to go to a foreign nation to help people if it meant not being in some sort of "civilized" place. As time went on, His desires became my desires. It was during this trip that the Lord used this opportunity to humble me yet further. After I returned, I got a construction job with a small company and was working on demolishing a kitchen one day. I was using my former abilities in Tae Kwon Do to help destroy this old kitchen with my foot. When I woke up the next morning my foot was in some pain. It felt fractured maybe, but

I wasn't sure. If I pushed on the area, it didn't hurt. It only hurt when I walked on it. I went to have it X-rayed and nothing appeared wrong. But the pain got worse and worse in only 4 days, to the point where I could hardly walk. My parents had flown out for my cousin's wedding, which I was to stand up in. The pain spread from my right foot to my right knee, and then to my left knee and left foot. It rendered me incapable of walking, literally. We went to the doctor and he couldn't figure it out, but gave me cortisone pills for 5 days. This helped tremendously and I thought I was ok. But as the wedding approached, the pain got worse and worse, as the cortisone pack was almost gone. I stood up in the wedding in much pain. That evening, I got in bed and never left the bed for the entire next month. The only time I was out of bed was to use the bathroom, see the doctor, go to my weekly prayer meeting, and occasionally go to the kitchen for food. I had to be driven to the doctor and even the prayer meetings, because the pain was so great that I couldn't even drive. By God's grace my parents were in town for about 2 full weeks, and they took care of me. At times they had to walk me to the bathroom due to the intense pain of being on my feet. The bathroom was only 10 feet off the end of my bed. Even while sleeping, the pain was quite intense. After they left, I had to fend for myself.

This was a very trying time for me, to say the least. The doctors didn't know what was wrong with me, and I was wrestling with the fact that I may never walk again. I didn't pray much and I certainly didn't read the Bible. I was in too much pain nearly constantly to do either. I just watched television during the month of July while the birds were chirping and the weather was gorgeous outside. All my friends were out having fun. Life could get worse, but not by much, I remember thinking. I had no job because I had quit the construction job after finding out that the Christian man didn't run his business so uprightly, it seemed. The money was running out with no prospects for a job anytime soon. My health and future walking abilities were now questionable. And I was still single and wishing God would bless me with my future wife before the rapture came. I really hated life and was really questioning God's plan for me. I didn't sign up for this, nor did I want it. I did everything under the sun to rebuke Satan and any demon that may be causing this illness; pray for health and healing, ask others to pray for me, but nothing changed. At the end of the month, my doctor sent me to an internal medicine doctor who diagnosed me with Reiter's syndrome. It's a form of arthritis that has a genetic marker in your blood, which I of course had. The good news was we knew what it was; the bad news was it may reoccur again at any time. The doctor who diagnosed me knew I had no job or insurance and waved his $200 office visit fee because he felt bad for me. Not only was I unemployed for several months, but now he gave me news of a condition I now had to live with. I appreciated it very much, but remember shedding some tears when I left the office, wondering what my future held now. Life continued to go downhill.

After seeing the arthritis doctor, I started on medications that allowed me to walk with significantly less pain. It took nearly 8 more months before I was completely healed and could start playing sports again. I do not believe it will return, but that's ultimately in God's hands. Still, the experience gave me a great appreciation for the elderly or anyone with arthritis–but more importantly, compassion for people who are sick to a much greater degree than I had ever had before. I have prayed for the gift of healing, and I believe that this is one reason why I went through that trying time in my life. Down the line, I can minister in love and compassion as Jesus did to the sick. **"Therefore, since Christ suffered in his body, arm yourselves also with the same attitude, because he who has suffered in his body is done with sin" (1Peter 4:1).**

It was after the third month of my arthritis condition that my finances were yet again on my mind. My grandmother needed a lot of work done in Chicago on her house. I decided to drive to Chicago on Sept 12th, 2001. Little did I know that Sept 11, 2001 was going to be the largest terrorist attack ever on this country. I put the trip off an extra day because I had heard some gas stations were price gouging. I didn't want to spend a lot more money trying to get to Chicago. I drove 19 hours the first day to Colorado and spent a couple days with my cousin. Then I drove another 16 hours to Chicago. Once there, I started work on my grandmother's house. She had a roof to repair, painting to be done, doors and windows to replace, and a lot of little things to do. If anyone has had or has arthritis now, you know that the barometric pressure really makes a big difference in how your joints feel. There were days where I could barely take the pain, even with the pain medication. Other days I was good. I remember one night sitting on the couch after working all day. I was almost in tears because the pain was so great. I said to my parents, "I don't think I can take another day of this pain or I'll lose it!" It's interesting because the next day onward, the pain was significantly less and was never bad like that again. I continued to improve and be completely healed over the next 4 months. I firmly believe the Lord heard me and the roughest part of that test was now over. This is not to imply that when we think we are at our lowest the test is nearly over. Often times it's not. But at least for that particular test and time, it was over.

I decided to return back to California about 1 month after I arrived in Chicago. Being away from home for too long makes me a bit edgy, especially since I have mail and bills that need tending to, and just life in general. I had planned it so that I would make the Monday night prayer meeting back in California if I pushed it. I left Chicago at 1am Sunday morning after only 2 hours of sleep. It was about 5am in Iowa when I came over a hill in the dark. Out of nowhere, my headlights saw a deer standing on the centerline of the road. The deer was approximately 85 feet from my truck. It wasn't until the headlights hit its legs that I saw him. There was no real time to do anything at that point. It all happened so fast, and yet so slow. I was traveling too fast to really turn the truck at all, because I knew at that speed I would roll the truck easily. He was facing away from me with his head turned backwards, looking towards me. As I approached, he started to turn around and into my lane of traffic to run! I remember thinking, oh my God, I'm going to nail him and I'm going to die from the impact! I think I must have had fur stuck to my back bumper because as he spun around to run across my lane of traffic, I passed him as he was leaning into my truck to run across the road. It all happened so fast. Even before I got to him, I saw him leaning in my direction to run. This made it more amazing to me that he never touched my truck as I passed by him! Even looking back, I find it hard to believe that he missed me. It seemed as though he passed through the truck without touching me. I know that's a far stretch–God only knows–but it was miraculous that nothing happened! My heart raced and raced. I sat and thanked God for quite sometime for His miraculous protection in that moment! I often wonder, how many other times in life God has rescued us when we had no idea we were in danger at all?

That day I drove 22 hours to the state line of eastern Nevada, where I had a reservation made at a local hotel and went to bed. That last hour on the salt flats in Utah I was nearly falling asleep. The next day I drove the remaining 10 hours home and made my prayer meeting at 7pm. The Lord spoke this word to me that evening:

My son, you would travel across this land.

You would step in your car and you would set a destination, and you would drive.

For you, the trip would be long, and yet I tell you, there are those who have taken the same trip, there are those, who, from another time, have traveled as you have traveled; and what took you days, it would take them weeks, it would take them months, for they would travel by foot...they would not have your car; and in this day this trip would seem long to you, for you have traveled by plane before, you know how quickly the distance can be traveled, and yet this time you would drive and it would seem long.

And so it is in life my son that people would travel the same distance, they would take the same trip, and for some it would take but hours, for others it would take days, and yet still others the trip would be long and laborious it would take weeks and months, and it would drain their very life to reach the destination.

Such is life my son, such is the life that people have lived, and such is your life my son, that some things would come easy and they would come quickly and yet others would be hard.

It would seem they would never come.

It would seem like you would never reach your destination.

Always it is further ahead, always it is in the distance, though you would see it in your mind, though you would desire it in your heart, yet it eludes you my son.

It is but a trip I tell you, it is the journey, and it is a journey that you will travel, for such is your life my son, that these are my words to you:

That you do not take a single step that I have not gone before you.

There is not a single place you would go that I would not go with you; and always my son I love you and I prepare the way, and I have made the road on which you travel.

I have chosen the destination.

I have determined that you would walk or you would fly.

It is of my doing my son, it is in my love, let this be your faith:

That I love you my son, even as you would be in the car and the land would stretch forth before you and you would see the distance is great, yet I love you.

Yet I sustain you.

Yet I protect you.

And such is your life my son that always I sustain you.

I love you, I protect you, and I make the way my son.

I make the way for you.

Do not lose hope, do not give up, for I love you my son, I have never lost hope in you, I have never given up in you.

Always I would seek to perfect you, to draw you to my side that you would see my face; you would look deep in my eyes and then you will see the love and you will know my son.

Do not give up, do not fear.

Know that I love you.

Know that I will make the way, and trust that the way will be easy.

Trust my son, it is not the footpath for you.

It is not the long trip for you.

I will make a way for you my son, I will make a way for you.

For about the last 2 years of my 4 years of unemployment, I started my own handyman business in California After my first trip to Mexico where I co-led the construction effort with my good friend Denis, several people from the church started asking me to fix things and do other handyman and construction related jobs. It was only after another year and another Mexico trip when the same thing happened that I decided to make it official and start my own business. Over that time I did nearly every job a house can have done to it, which taught me a lot about construction and repairs, beyond what I had already done. I had been doing minor things since I was 16 and had always been interested in construction. When people ask me where I learned the skills I have, I always told them I used to watch a lot of "This Old House" and other shows like it since. It is the truth; television taught me a lot. I can also watch someone do something and know how to do it just by watching them. I also went on 11 more trips to Mexico. I led and co-led teams of construction people on small houses, orphanages, the church, and a two story house for the junior pastor, which was my favorite. I hope to do more of this type of work in the future. The reward of seeing a family in tears of joy for something that they could never afford on their own is far better than almost anything I've ever experienced. God gifts each one of us with different abilities and talents. Once we turn our lives to Him, He uses those things to advance His kingdom. I should also say that the things you enjoy doing most, God will often create circumstances for your service that you could have never dreamed of yourself. It's exciting, fun and rewarding! "**For we are God's workmanship, created in Christ Jesus to do good works, which God prepared in advance for us to do" (Ephesians 2:10).**

During that time, the money I made as a handyman was quite good, except that I didn't do it 40 hours a week. Jobs were few and far between for the most part. My finances were gone completely after about 1 year of unemployment from software. I told the Lord after I quit my job that I would continue to give the same amounts to ministry that I had been giving until the money ran out. The money ran out on a Sunday morning at church. I put the last $5 I had in this world into the offering bucket as I left. I remember telling the Lord, "Ok, I held up my end of the deal. Now it's your turn." It's one thing to talk about how much you have faith or believe the Lord; it's quite another to have to live it out. That's where the "rubber meets the road" as far as your faith is concerned.

I owed about $500 in bills by the end of that coming week, and I had nothing left to pay them. I got on my knees and fasted and prayed for 4 days. It was on the fourth day that out of the blue, 2 different people I knew gave me over $1,300. One of them knew my situation, the other did not. I know some may be saying, "Well that's nice and all, but God didn't do anything. Someone else felt sorry for you and gave it to you." I agree with that if you think in the natural, but when you know the one true Living God, nothing happens by accident or coincidence. God either allows bad things to happen to teach, test, and try you, or by your own sin and disobedience bad things may happen. Before I was a Christian, my logic used to think the same way. I have a very logical engineering mindset. The Lord once told me that unless He had allowed disaster to come into my life, I would have never turned to Him or known Him. I firmly believe that. God used many testimonies of others to strengthen my faith for the financial trials I was now experiencing. Without them, I don't think I would have believed enough in Him to get through it all.

Looking back, I cannot even begin to figure out how I made it through the last four years financially. There were so many times where the money somehow, someway came in, and I was able to pay my bills. One job I took was re-roofing my friend's roof. We agreed on the price and it was getting close to the end of the month. I remember praying for exactly $2,000, which I needed to pay my mortgage. Even though I knew what I was getting paid, I thought I had gotten paid more than I had so far. It was 3 days before the money was due, and she told me she still owed me a balance of $1,700. It may sound dumb, but because I didn't realize she owed me so much still, God came through for me once again. I've learned this lesson so often–to trust in the Lord even in the face of major obstacles–and yet, I still occasionally do not trust. We are human, after all, and full of weakness until the Lord takes us home. **Proverbs 3:5–6** is one of my favorite verses. It says, **"Trust in the Lord with all your heart and lean not on your own understanding; in all your ways acknowledge him, and he will make your paths straight."**

Another time I was working on a big handyman job at a woman's house. I had bid a portion of the job to remove concrete for her before she had a professional concrete company come in and pour new concrete. The concrete company was actually owned by my friend. It was a good thing, because when I got into the job I realized there was no way to finish it anytime soon with the tools I had rented. I also had ordered a concrete waste bin, which I had paid for already. Things were getting ugly very quickly when I realized I couldn't do it. By Gods grace, I called my friend and we negotiated part of the price off his side of things for the trash bin. He also discounted the price for his company to finish the demolition for which she was going to pay me. On top of that good news, I was counting on the nearly $800 I was going to receive from finishing this job to pay bills 5 days later. This was a common thread during most of that time, receiving money shortly before it was due. As I left the job after negotiating with my friend on his price and the situation, I prayed to the Lord. I said, "Lord, you know I needed this money. I have no idea how you're going do it this time for me, but I trust you." Amazingly, when I got home I had a message on my

Jeff Lacki

answering machine for another job. It not only paid the $800 I needed short term, but over the next 2 months brought in more than $2,000 in additional work!

Things often went like that. Just when I saw no future in finances, God came through for me in small ways or larger ways. It was always up and down. Don't get me wrong; there were times when I was late on bills and it bothered me a lot. I was particularly worried about my good credit scores. I often didn't pay my mortgage until the 15th or even after many times. My parents were on my case constantly about possibly selling the house and moving someplace cheaper. Honestly, Satan was trying to get to me through their doubt, fear and unbelief. Not that they don't know the Lord, but we all have different measures of faith. I told them many times that they needed to stop saying those things and that Satan was using them to get to me. They were just very concerned of course. Satan will very often work through the people closest to you because he knows that those same people have the most influence over you. Peter was used by Satan to tell Jesus He would not go to the Cross. Jesus rebuked Satan in Peter, **Matthew 16:23**.

The Lord had told me not to move time and time again, both through the Word and also through my close Christian friends. It was quite difficult to stay focused on God's plan for me with my parents and peer pressure telling me to move. Persecution comes in all sorts of ways. Very often it comes through the very people who love you most. The most amazing part of all of this was when I went to buy another home here in Phoenix and my credit score was checked, I still had perfect credit! That testimony alone still amazes me!

I often say to some Christian friends how I find

more faith in non-believers sometimes than I do in people who claim to be true believers in Christ. We are all human and imperfect; however, we need to think before we speak. I'm just as guilty of this as the next person at times. We need to understand just how much power our words can carry. Blessings and cursing come from us at times even when we may not realize it. This is a topic for yet another book.

With the Lord directing me to stay put, my mind began to wonder about where I would live long-term in San Jose once this long trial was over. If I found a wife and had a family, there would be no room for us all in my small house. I loved my neighbors and my neighborhood. I really couldn't have picked a better neighborhood to live in. I know it was the Lord even though when I purchased the home, I wasn't saved yet. One evening at a prayer meeting, I was thinking about this. I had the idea to rebuild my home from the ground up. After all, the land was the most expensive part. I knew that I could do the job myself and save a lot of money. I also had all the time in the world to work on the project, and it was the best time ever to re-finance a home. Over the next week I prayed a lot about this. One evening at another prayer meeting, the Lord spoke this word to me:

My son, you would speak of your home, and you would consider plans that you would expand your home and place new rooms within it - and what is old would be made new.

These are plans for your home, my son, and yet I tell you that you also are my home; that I live in you and even as you would remodel your home, even as you would expand your home, even as what is old would be made new, yet that is my desire for you.

That as I would live in you, yet I would expand you, my son; you would be greater than you were before, and what is old within you I will renew and I will make new, my son.

My desire, my son, is not for the house within which you live, but for the house within which I live, that I would make a new work - a new work in you, my son.

So these are my words to you:

Continue in your ways, my son.

Continue upon your path, for truly your journey leads to Me.

Truly, my son, my desire is that you would continue to grow and to learn and to have more of Me in your life.

And are these not also your prayers?

Is this not also your heart?

And have I not given you this heart?

For truly it is my heart as well.

And these are my words:

That as I seek to build - it shall be built.

And what I build will not be torn down.

You will be made new, my son.

My home shall be built and I will build it with my Spirit and I will build it in you.

After this word, I was still unsure if God was saying yes or no. After all, that was the question I was asking. After keeping it in prayer and moving forward to investigate permits and other costs, I realized that it was not possible to do what I wanted, for various reasons. My plan had been to re-finance the house and pull some money out to do the project. My thoughts then turned towards doing something I had always wanted to do even since I was little; learn how to fly. I knew that money was tight. I hedged on my future by pulling cash out of the house, both to live on and pay off some debt that had been accumulating. I had figured enough money to last me 1 year. I also added in some money to learn how to fly, and so I did. In the midst of this trial and suffering, I was able to do what I had always wanted to do. I added this side note because looking back, I find that the Lord does that in our lives. Maybe not to the extent that I have shown here, but there are things in our lives that are beautiful even in the midst of the trial. There are things that are in your life that are still a blessing, no matter how small, even if just the love of a good friend or spouse, or your health, or the fact that you have food and fresh water. Many people in the world do not even have these basic things. Satan is always trying to focus our attention on our problems or lack. We need to stay focused on the Lord. He is truly all we need. He already has a plan; we just need to sit with Him and trust in Him always. Again, **Jeremiah 29:11**. I've realized time and time again that the blessings in my life far outweigh what I don't have. Let's face it, things can always be worse. I also find that the deeper the valley, the greater the blessing that is awaiting you on the other side of the valley if you persevere. I know for sure that in Heaven, God will right all wrongs. No matter how bad your life is or was, He shall reward you if you are faithful to Him and believe in Him. If God were not just and fair, we should all go out and get everything we can because there would be no even ground ever. We need to remember, our hope is always in Jesus, always! This world isn't worth living in apart from Him.

It always seemed as though things got brighter for a while financially, then they dried up just as quickly as things started to go well. Towards the end of 2003, business was picking up so much that I thought it was never going to end. Countless people were calling me for work, both small and large jobs. As Christmas approached, job after job started drying up or not coming to pass. By January 2004, I had nothing at all once again. January and February would be my darkest days. I had no work and no money at all. The depression I had had on and off would be nothing compared to how it was about to be during those two months. Satan started hitting me hard, telling me the Lord was never going to answer me or help me. It was hopeless and things were never going to change. I had a hard time rejecting those thoughts because of the pain and suffering I was going through. For as strong as the Lord has made us, sometimes we feel like we are the weakest Christian around when God is working in our lives. Thoughts of suicide started in as well. I remember one very bad day walking around the house like there was absolutely no hope left in this world. Having no extra money for so long rendered my life almost useless to do much of anything, like go to a movie or just even out with my friends. Plus with so much time on my hands from boredom, all I was doing was living day to day as I had when I was recovering from my broken relationship. Only this time, I had no job to occupy part of my time, or money to do anything extra. I remember one day leaning against the wall in my living room with no hope left in me and depression gripping my heart. I remember God speaking very clearly to my heart as I really thought about suicide. I was so deeply depressed, the kind of depression that comes on you when your circumstance appears to be unending. He asked me three questions. He said, "If I gave you a million dollars today, tax free in your bank account, would that make you happy?" I thought about it for a moment and realized that money wasn't the entire issue. I said, "No, that wouldn't make me happy."

Next He asked, "If I gave you a wife right now, would that make you happy?" I thought for a few seconds and said, "No that wouldn't make me happy either." He then asked me, "What would make you happy?" I realized more than I had ever before at that moment that nothing in this world really would make me happy, at least in the natural. Yes, a wife and a million dollars would certainly go a long way to end my depression, but I realized more than ever in that moment that God was showing me how He is the true source of all happiness and joy. Without Him, I am nothing and have nothing. It's true that having money does go a long way to allowing us to "live it up" in whatever sense that is for us; however, I remember having a lot of money years before and still being deeply lonely and depressed inside. Nothing in this world can ever fully fill the void that God put in our heart for Him when He created us–nothing. It's unfortunate that most people have to find that out the hard way first.

Those revelations about God were true, but momentary for me. In mid February my aunt, who had been waiting for someone else to do some major work at her house in Chicago, spoke with me and told me that nothing ever came of this person doing the work for her. She asked if I would be interested in coming to Chicago to do the work. Seeing as how I was desperately broke and about $5,000 behind on my bills already, I prayed about this with a friend. The Lord said yes, go to Chicago. It was also rather obvious that the Lord had held that job for me. My aunt had been waiting on this person for 3 months. Every time it appeared he would come by and give an estimate, something always happened and he never came over. The following week, my dad flew out to California to drive back with me. We drove two very long days back to Chicago. Once in Chicago, I had to order cabinets for her kitchen, which can take several weeks to get. My aunt and I ordered the cabinets. From there I drove down to Tennessee to do some work for my Christian friends who had moved there several months earlier. I spent a week there, and I believe it was Gods Grace that sent me. After all the depression and loneliness of the prior 2 months, I snapped. I became bitterly angry with God as I arrived in Tennessee. I told my friends how angry I was and how I didn't much care anymore to follow the Lord. I completely believed that the Lord is real, don't misunderstand me. But there are times when we just want to return to the world because we can't take it any longer. The loneliness I felt within my soul was more than I could bear any longer. Whether that meant a girlfriend or just plain sex, I didn't care at that point in some ways. This was how I was feeling to be very honest. I have to laugh when non-believers say how easy it is to be a "Chrisitan" and add how weak-minded we are. If you are truly following Jesus Christ, your life will be harder than if you stayed in the world, for several reasons. In the end however, our eternal life will be beyond description for being faithful to the Lord! How I wish (figuratively speaking) that I had such an "easy" life as a non-believer at times. This is, of course, a general statement.

These were the same friends who discipled me and were in ministry with me for several years. I believe God sent me there at that exact time so they could pray with me and for me. I was pretty mad, but by the end of the week I felt better. I realized that I was being completely oppressed and attacked by Satan. Still, it wasn't easy to feel so great towards God. After all, He has the power to stop our trial at anytime He chooses, which is why I have often gotten angry with Him, incorrectly of course. I also realized I had come so far with the Lord. To turn my back now may mean prolonging my trial years longer, which I just couldn't take.

Satan came to tempt Jesus 3 times at His weakest hour just after spending 40 days in the desert, right after His baptism by John the Baptist (Luke 4). Jesus didn't say to Satan, "Do you know who I am? I'm Jesus, the son of God. How dare you come against me!" Instead, Jesus used the Word of God (The Bible) to rebuke Satan. The Word is also called the Sword of the Spirit (Ephesians 6:17). Notice also that Satan knows the Bible very well, as he quotes scripture to Jesus. It is our job also to know the Word deep within our hearts and use it as Satan comes against us. Jesus set the example for us to follow. My point here is that near or at the end of every trial is a great temptation.

I was strengthened enough after my week in Tennessee to go back to Chicago, continue my 2 month stay and finish my work. Satan still had a grip on me, but not nearly as much as he had before. While I was in Chicago, I had a small Bible study at my grandmother's house each week to help teach and encourage my relatives while I was home. I tried my best to stay the course. After returning home, I was planning on going on another Mexico mission trip to build another 2 homes. I drove home in 36 hours with only 3 hours of sleep at a couple truck stops in Nevada. This was partly because I needed to make it home for the trip to Mexico, and partly because I really missed my own home! This time I had no problems on the road at all. In fact, driving through Wyoming, there was a very dark storm ahead of me. As I drove through this storm and was coming out on the other side, the Lord spoke to me and told me that my life was also taking the same turn. I was coming out of the blackness of my trials and into the light of His blessings again. Nature is so awesome and can be so beautiful as well.

The trip to Mexico was such a blast, as they always are. I was so happy to be back home again, even if still broke. It was now spring in California and my grass was really high, as well as the weeds in my backyard! Some of the weeds in my backyard were over 5 feet tall. I couldn't believe it. Everything was in bloom. It was so awesome to be home! The good news was that I caught up enough on my bills to be slightly ahead. The bad news was that no work came in at all again, and Satan was still working on me to make me fall. This time, however, I was definitely stronger to rebuke him.

There's a verse in **Deuteronomy 7:22–23** that says, **"The Lord your God will drive out those nations before you, little by little. You will not be allowed to eliminate them all at once, or the wild animals will multiply around you. But the Lord your God will deliver them over to you, throwing them into great confusion until they are destroyed."** The "wild animals" and "nations" are demons. They represent all the powers of darkness that come against you. When you get saved, God does not eliminate them immediately because if He did, you would have no strength of your own to fight the enemy. Remember, we are warriors in a spiritual battle, not only sons and daughters of God. We will be at war until the day we die.

I had been borrowing a little bit of money from my parents ever since January. After the money ran out when I returned from Chicago, I borrowed more and more. I prayed a lot about what to do. Like most people, I don't like to borrow at all when possible. I was even angry at my good friend for suggesting that God was "starving me out" to get me to move. I told them that if God wanted me to move, all he had to do was tell me and I would! In the end, I think they were right, but I won't know until I get to heaven.

The months in between returning from Chicago and June were hard, but not nearly as hard as January and February had been. After being away from home so long and returning home to spring-time in California, I was really happy to be home and enjoying the gorgeous weather. I rode my bicycle several times a week. The Lord provided me with the time, so I made the most of the awesome weather and my ability to enjoy it as best I could. Keeping active suppressed the deep concerns in my heart over money. **Ephesians 6:13** says, **"Therefore put on the full armor of God, so that when the day of evil comes, you may be able to stand your ground, and after you have done everything, to stand."** At this point I had done everything to stand my ground against my enemy, so I did. I stood my ground and waited on the Lord for my next move in faith knowing it would come.

On June 7th, 2004 at our weekly prayer meeting at my house, the Lord spoke to us and said:

My children, I speak to you of the significance of what happened this evening, the declaration from my servant who said:

"At 7:45, the seventh day of June, 2004."

The reason for that my children is to establish a benchmark in each and every one of your lives, for this evening has a significance to Me - it should also be a significance to you, that as you move on into the future you will look back at this date that was declared and the time that was stated so that you will know that I have heard and that I have answered; it is for this reason and a purpose, for there is much more that is going to be accomplished in this place, for did not I declare in your midst in past days that there would be great and mighty things that would take place in this house?

And it is forth-coming my children, for I have declared it, I have willed it to be done.

So as you look back and remember, 7:45, the 7th day of June, 2004, you will see, that was the day and the hour and the moment when I started a new thing in your life.

So I ask that you will be faithful and obedient to the tasks that are before each and every one of you.

Each one are different...they will come together and you will see, they will have a reason and pur-pose in the future, and how I will use you because you are now moving into your destiny.

It has been foretold and proclaimed and willed from the foundation of the world, and your destiny is beginning to unfold, so therefore, the significance of what was declared on this day.

So I ask of each and every one of you to be faithful and obedient to the calling that I have on your lives and the anointing that shall go with it.

So remember, be faithful and obedient and I shall be with you to the very end.

I need to add something here. The "house" God was referring to was not my natural house, but each of us, for we are each the "house" and "temple" of God. **"If anyone destroys God's temple, God will destroy him; for God's temple is sacred, and you are that temple" (1Corinthians 3:17).**

My next door neighbors were moving to Sacramento about this time. It was during their packing up and getting ready to move that the Lord started to birth within me the idea of leaving San Jose. For several years He had told me not to leave California, contrary to my parents' advice and others. I really struggled over finally leaving. I told Him that unless he brought me a job or enough work to pay my bills, I was going to start planning on leaving California. I still wasn't sure if it was God or me, but as time went on I realized it really was God's idea birthed within my heart. I was leaving because I had no choice any longer. I had done my best to make money and survive, but nothing was happening anymore. I had already borrowed about $12K from my parents over the last 8 months trying to survive, and I knew that that wasn't a long term solution either. Besides, my home was worth over half a million dollars by now, and I lived in the one of the most expensive parts of the country. Moving anywhere else would be a step up, financially speaking.

As I looked at several cities to move to, I was also in the midst of preparing the house to sell, so I had a ton of work that still needed to be done. I had left many things unfinished until I had more money to complete them; however, now I had to do them so the house would be attractive to sell. The great part about this was that I love working on projects. It kept me occupied instead of being bored. It also gave me direction and focus for a change, plus my life was finally moving forward in the natural. I prayed a lot about where to move to. God spoke to me and said basically go where you want to go, and I will be with you and bless you there. When the house was finally complete and up for sale, I still didn't know for sure yet where I was going. I had a sense it was going to be either Sacramento or Phoenix. There were some reasons I chose those two places, but I kept seeking the Lord in that. The house wasn't selling for about 10 days. My realtor told me that about 1/3 of the people were saying how they loved the house except the kitchen needed to be completely remodeled, which was true. It hadn't been touched in probably 20 years. I was in Sacramento at my cousin's house for a weekend birthday party and told my realtor that if it didn't sell by Saturday evening, I was driving home on Sunday morning to rip out the kitchen and remodel it within the week. Amazingly in less than 2 hours, I got a phone call back that someone made me a solid offer on the house. Within 30 minutes of that first phone call, I had signed and faxed the paperwork and the house was sold! The funny thing was I still didn't know where I was going, and now I had about 3.5 weeks to leave the house. I felt like Abraham did when God said pick up and go and I will show you where to go, yet he had no idea where he was going.

It was a slightly scary time, but at the same time I kept telling myself that God was in control. I had no doubt He was, but as a human being, I hate discomfort; we all do. I think most of us like to be in control of our lives as well. It's only in discomfort that we grow and stretch, and our faith grows in the Lord. I had to wait seven days until the deal with the new buyer became solid enough where I could purchase another home. During those seven days, I made up my mind to move to Phoenix, Arizona. I felt it made the most sense and held the best prospects for a future for me. At the end of those seven days, I drove down to Arizona and spent 3 days there with my cousin to purchase a home. I had already looked around in Sacramento and the prices were still too high. Plus the software job market wasn't as good as in Phoenix. The first day out in Phoenix, my realtor and I found a great little home that I ended up purchasing to be a future rental property until I figured out where I was going to live and get myself settled. Exactly two weeks later, both homes closed on the same day. I left California and immediately moved into the home in Phoenix. Again, God was really blessing me and making the way easy. I had dreaded having to move all my stuff twice!

After a month of fixing up the house I had just purchased, I had been looking at new homes in the Phoenix area for a future move. Everything had a waiting list or lottery, plus a build time of 9 months to 1 year in most cases. I stumbled into an area that my realtor took me to. I wasn't even keen on the location or area but we went into the models anyhow. It just so happened they had 2 homes that people had backed out on that were already well under construction. They both had been on the market for 7 days, which is pretty rare here in Phoenix lately as the market is very hot! I went home and prayed about it, and the next morning decided to purchase it as another investment opportunity. I still wanted to buy another house in about 1 more year and make the third house the house that I planned to be at permanently. As it turns out, I beat another buyer by 15 minutes the next morning when I went to sign the paperwork and make my deposit. They were not too happy. I've since decided to stay in this location for other reasons for now. I also had a pool and hot tub built in the backyard, something else my heart has always desired!

As I finish this book, I'm very excited to see how God blesses me with a wife in the very near future, as well as ministry and new friends. Even in the midst of this financial blessing, it has been hard–due to loneliness and being in a new city–not knowing almost anyone. This is yet a continuation of my former trials; however, I still know how good the Lord is. He shall bless me with these things as well. I am still unemployed, but that too shall change soon. I'm not sure what the Lord wants me to do yet, though I do believe writing more books, speaking and ministering will definitely be in the plan somehow. I have a great expectation of what my future holds for me through Christ!

The same week the publishers of this book called me and said they wanted to publish this book, the Lord completely delivered me of my sexual addiction, which I talk more about later in this book. I had prayed for over 3.5 years to be delivered of this addiction. How do I know it was the Lord, you may ask? All I can say is that all of a sudden, the desires that had been driving me to sin lifted from me in a single day. I no longer desired those sins anymore. As of this writing, about

5 months have gone by and I am completely set free! **"So if the Son sets you free, you will be free indeed" (John 8:36).** I have also started to connect with other Christians in the area. Life is starting to get busy again. Other ministry opportunities seem to be opening up now. I believe I'm being led to write a second book already. In all things, good or bad, the Lord is *always* good to those who are faithful and love Him! The greatest rewards await each of us as we patiently endure this world for the world to come! **Galations 6:9** says **"Let us not become weary in doing good, for at the proper time we will reap a harvest if we do not give up."**

Count the Cost

In **Luke 14**, Jesus speaks about the cost of being his disciple. He also states in **John 16:33 "In this world you will have trouble. But take heart! I have overcome the world."** Let's face it; whether you are a believer in Christ or not, you have times and seasons of suffering in your life. They can be great or small, long or short. The good news for the believer in Christ is that you aren't suffering without a reason. All suffering is there for a reason and purpose in your life to bring about the Godly and Holy life God desires for you to live. For the unbeliever, it's just suffering. There is no reward associated with it. God is possibly trying to get your attention through your suffering. Or it could just be that you are suffering because you don't have God's hand upon your life, and Satan has brought it about. Either way, without Christ, you are just suffering. There is no reward for it or benefit to you other than to suffer. Kind of sucks, doesn't it? **1Peter 5:8** says, **"Your enemy the devil prowls around like a roaring lion looking for someone to devour."** Satan is constantly looking for an opportunity to "devour" a human being who God has created, but who does not know the Lord or walks in His covering. We are under God's divine covering once we are a born again believer. If not, we are under a curse until we turn our life to Christ. **"If anyone does not love the Lord—a curse be on him" (1Corinthians 16:22).** Don't be misled into thinking that just because you feel or seem blessed you are not living under a curse. This world is cursed due to the fall of man. The curse many live under will eventually be revealed in their lives unless they turn and follow the Lord. I don't say this as a threat of course, just as a spiritual fact.

The cost of following Jesus can, at times, be quite difficult. **John 15:20** says **"'No servant is greater than his master.' If they persecuted me, they will persecute you also. If they obeyed my teaching, they will obey yours also."** Persecution comes in many forms. Some bold and in your face, some subtle and not so easily recognizable, and sometimes, not even known to you. If you've read any of the Gospels, the greatest persecutors of Jesus and his disciples were the church of the day, the Pharisees and Sadducees. I'm sure there were others who were against them, but it seems to be emphasized more than not that the persecution was from the church authority of the time. They were jealous of Jesus and worried about losing control over the people. They enjoyed having the best seats in the synagogue and being greeted in the marketplaces. They loved their "status" and didn't want Jesus "hogging in" on their "action." Even Herod, when he was told that the prophesied Messiah was born by the Magi, ordered all babies under 2 years old killed in that region. He later found out the Magi had deceived him (**Matthew 2**). In today's churches, there are those who misuse their God given authority. Many people have been overlooked for ministry opportunities and other such positions. The Lord knows and will reward them ultimately. Other persecution comes from one's own family and friends, or even neighborhood or workplace. Even in my short time with the last software position here in Phoenix I was told not to speak about religion by my boss. Satan constantly confirms what I am doing against his kingdom is having an effect. When I was first saved my family thought

I was in a cult because I seemed to change overnight and so radically. I know it was out of love for me that most of them felt this way and were concerned. Even as time has gone by and they have come to know that I'm not in a cult, some still say things behind my back about what I'm doing and who my friends are in the Christian community. These things are really nothing to me in the grand scheme of things. Even Jesus said, **"Only in his hometown and in his own house is a prophet without honor" (Matthew 13:57).** I'm not a prophet just yet, but the point is that among those who know you, you are misunderstood and without honor as you grow in and follow the Lord. These people grew up with Jesus. They knew Jesus firsthand. **"'Where did this man get these things?' they asked. 'What's this wisdom that has been given him, that he even does miracles! Isn't this the carpenter? Isn't this Mary's son and the brother of James, Joseph, Judas and Simon? Aren't his sisters here with us?' And they took offense at him" (Matthew 13:54–57).** Granted, I'm not a miracle worker yet either, or anyone so great and wonderful as Jesus obviously. But these words are true even for the brand new baby in Christ. Many of us have many testimonies of how our closest friends, family, relatives, and co-workers were and are offended by our faith in Christ.

At one point quite a while after I was saved, the Lord told me that my ex girlfriend broke up with me because of Him and not her lack of love for me. Looking back, that was true. Just before I left and gave my heart to the Lord, she started saying things like, "I hope you aren't going to mention God to people because it's embarrassing how much you are starting to do this now." I couldn't help myself. God was doing His work in me. I was along for the ride, so to speak.

The world will hate you because of Jesus, but that's ok; it's supposed to. After all, Satan is currently the head of this world, and **"He who is not with me is against me, and he who does not gather with me scatters" (Matthew 12:30, Luke 11:23)** Jesus said. Even if you are an unbeliever and are not actively opposed to Christians or Christ, Jesus says here you "scatter" by default. That is, you are against His Kingdom. Let's face it: If you don't stand for something, you aren't standing for anything. In **Revelation 3:15–16**, to the church of Laodicea it says, **"I know your deeds, that you are neither cold nor hot. I wish you were either one or the other! So, because you are lukewarm—neither hot nor cold—I am about to spit you out of my mouth."**

The following words I added here in which the Lord mentions lukewarmness.

This word came January 12, 2001 after we had been singing a song that says "let it be a sweet, sweet sound in your ears."

My children, what I have been hearing is truly a sweet sound in my ears. It has risen up into my throne room in that place that I declared where the prayers of the saints would be collected.

Did not I say in my Word that it would be mixed with incense and would come before Me; and it would be pleasant and pleasing to Me and then the declaration should come from my lips and I would send those prayers back to earth, and the impact that it would make on earth because those prayers were released.

Take comfort my children, take comfort in what has transpired this evening to this point.

I encourage you to do this often, more so than what you are currently doing now, for is it not the time when its needed to assemble yourselves together often and do this?

Did not the church that was established many years ago in its early stages gather itself together often because it saw the need?

My children, that need is before you now.

Understand the dynamics that is necessary for meeting together often in this manner.

Coming before Me and offering your prayers, your requests, your supplications.

For I'm hearing, I'm desiring, and I place that desire within you and I say to you, I say to you again....MEET-OFTEN....Meet often and gather yourselves together, whether it be two or three, but I declare to you...MEET-TOGETHER-OFTEN, for it is necessary and it is a requirement for you to stand true in the days ahead.

For it is in this manner that I shall show you and direct you and guide you and to help you to be overcomers.

For that is my desire my children, that you become overcomers to the very end.

Precious promises have been declared in my Word to those who will stay true and overcome to the end.

But also be concerned about those who will stumble and fall.

Did not I say in my Word that there will be those who shall fall away from the faith?

Let that not be declared of you my children.

But as you do that amongst yourselves, reach out for others, grab a hold of their hand, encourage them, for in so doing you will strengthen them and they will not fall away from the faith when the pressure comes in the days ahead.

For surely, my children, it-shall-come!

For judgement must come, and I declare that to you.

Judgement must first begin in my house and then I will then move into the rest of the world.

So you will need that my children, you will need that to comfort one another, to build one another in the most holy faith.

You will need that for yourselves as well as others.

Consider, consider what it is.

Look into what they did in the New Testament church.

Consider what you will need to do in the days ahead as things begin to unfold.

For it is my plan and my purposes that are being fulfilled.

That I forewarn you now, prepare yourself.

Prepare yourself, strengthen yourself for the days ahead, for they are troublesome my children, they are troublesome, like the world has never seen.

For I am moving, and I am preparing a people.

Did not I say that I no longer will be satisfied with lukewarmness?

I am now moving to make them either hot or cold.

So prepare yourself for what is coming, for it is

my Word and it shall be fulfilled before your very eyes in the days ahead.

Then in January 2002 the Lord said:

I've been listening this evening as you have been talking and speaking of revival, and truly that is in my plan and purpose for my children, that they would be revived in the days ahead to serve Me in a greater measure than what they ever had in the past; but I want to speak to you this evening my children that with that anticipation of the revival coming.

I say to you get ready for persecution.

For Satan does not want this, because he's your arch-enemy and he does not want this to happen.

He does not want the significance of this revival to flow through your land, and not just your land but around the world.

And so he will fight and he will resist.

So think it not strange my children that you are rejoicing in the revival that it will come, and your heart will be stirred up and rejoicing in the fact that revival has come.

Think it not strange that those who have named my name to you will not rejoice with you.

For is this not the time and the season when I will do the separation?

Have not I said in my Word that there shall be the separation of the wheat and the tears, the sheep and the goat?

Did not I also say that there will be the hot and the cold?

I will no longer be satisfied with the lukewarm.

The time is coming my children, sooner than you think, when this demarcation shall take place, and *it shall be very defined, and you shall see with your eyes unfolding before you who are the true believers and who have just been saying that they are believers.*

For it is the days ahead that shall test and try and show to you who are the true worshippers who want to worship Me in spirit and in truth.

You shall see by the hunger in their heart, the thirsting after righteousness.

For this is what I shall do, I shall stir and I shall fan the fire that is within those people, and it shall get hotter and hotter and hotter; and you shall see the results of that.

You shall see the willingness of my people to go forth, to be ambassadors, to be witnesses, to tell the good news, for this is the ear-mark of those who are following after Me, their desire to give the gospel, the good news, of what My Son has done at Calvary for them.

So this is my word to you my children, this evening.

With it, be prepared for the persecution that shall come, and do not be surprised, the persecution and the sources that will bring it to you.

Do not be surprised, for I am not surprised, and that is why I am saying to you this evening:

Be prepared my children.

Get into the foundation of the Word.

Read my Word, for I have already declared in my Word what shall transpire in the days ahead.

For it is coming, it is coming my children, sooner than you think.

For with this move that I am moving around the

world, Satan will do his utmost to destroy it, to bring it down, to defame it, so get ready my children for the attacks, the attacks that shall come to you to try to deter you from giving this gospel, this good news that is being put into you, birthed in you, fanned in you, the fire that shall get hotter and hotter and hotter.

Be faithful my children and obedient to the end and I shall give you the rewards that are promised for being an overcomer.

And again in May 2002:

My children, I say to you this evening in what has been declared concerning lukewarmness is correct for I have put that prayer within each and every one of you so that you would know my heart; and the day has passed, I say that to you my children... the day has passed for lukewarmness.

The time for separation is before you, before your brothers and sisters in Christ, and so this message must be declared boldly my children - lukewarmness is no longer part for grace in that area has stopped.

And the time...the time has come and it is now, from this moment on when I will only accept hot or cold.

That is what I have declared in my Word and I declare to you this evening...from my lips to your hearing.

The time of grace for lukewarmness has stopped and it's either hot or cold.

This is what I am saying to you, and it's "Thus Saith the Lord God."

Very sobering words from the Lord, but all true and all contained in His Word concerning the days in which we live. Things seem to be moving much faster in the last couple years as it pertains to persecution, even within our own country.

Counting the cost to follow Jesus also means that we will be put through trials, and our faith will be tested on a continual basis. That doesn't mean that life is without joy or there aren't seasons of great blessing in our lives. It just means that God is always using circumstances to shape us into the image of Jesus Christ if we allow Him to work in our lives. If we resist, a trial may last far longer than it had to. The Israelites, from what I have been taught, could have made the journey to the promised land in 2 weeks. Instead, because of their unbelief, it took them 40 years. An entire generation died because of their fear, doubt and unbelief. If you aren't willing to count the cost to follow Christ, you will fall away unless you pray and ask the Lord to help you persevere. He *is* able to help you and deliver you *if* you believe. Do you believe? It is hard, but have faith and be encouraged! God is for you and not against you when you put your faith in Him. I always confess to Him that "I am weak" when it comes to standing for Christ. Only by His power and strength can I stand firm! My prayer has always been for His strength in my life; I cannot do it on my own.

Several years ago I met a Christian woman who I really liked. I had been praying for several weeks about her. One night at our prayer meeting, I was asking the Lord about her. I prayed, "Not my will but yours be done in this situation." The Lord then spoke this word to me:

My son, you have asked for my will, just as the will of my Son was to do my will.

And in agony in the garden he prayed that this cup would be removed "But not my will but your will be done."

And according to my plans he went to the Cross.

For the joy that was put before him he withstood the agony on the Cross; he poured forth His blood for the redemption of mankind.

And now you, my son, are asking not my will be done but your will be done, and this pleases Me.

And just as my Son put his will down and picked up the Cross that his joy would be full, you shall see this too, my son.

You shall have your joy because you have put my will before yours.

We need to always remember to put God's will for our lives ahead of our own. It is only then that we will live out His perfect plan for our life and overcome all that tries to destroy us in this world.

Forgiveness

Forgiveness is probably one of the most difficult things we all face in our walk with the Lord. Sometimes the wounds are so deep that it would appear impossible for some. Who of us has *never* had someone hurt us deeply? Or just hurt us in general? We all have, to one degree or another. I have been quite fortunate that I did not grow up in an abusive home or have any large tragedies befall me at the hands of other people thus far in my life. What many people do not know or understand is that forgiveness is essential in our walk with the Lord. In the Lord's Prayer in **Matthew 6:12** it says, **"Forgive us our debts (*sins*) as we also have forgiven our debtors (*those who sinned against us*)."** In this prayer, we are *praying* that God will forgive us as we forgive others who sin against us. When we come to Christ, we ask the Lord to forgive us our sins. An unbeliever is not forgiven his or her sins because they have not asked for it and believed in Jesus Christ. If we, who are in Christ, do not forgive *anyone* who sins against us, God shall not forgive us either as stated in that prayer. It goes on to say: **"For if you forgive men when they sin against you, your heavenly Father will also forgive you. But if you do not forgive men their sins, your Father will not forgive you your sins" (Matthew 6:14–15).**

Un-forgiveness also keeps you in spiritual bondage. Jesus came to set you free! Jesus does not want you living in bondage. He came to give you life and give it to the fullest! **"I have come that they may have life, and have it to the full" (John 10:10).**

What good does it do you if you hold a grudge towards someone who cut you off on the road? They may not even realize they cut you off. If you hold onto the bitterness, anger, and revenge in your spirit, it will eat at you–whether for a few seconds or days depending on how you handle this and other circumstances in your life. This may be true of someone you are holding a grudge against who said something about you or offended you in some way. They may not even know they hurt you. Or it may have been a misunderstanding. Satan *loves* to sow these seeds of un-forgiveness in our hearts so we will be separated from God.

Remember, sin separates us from God the Father. It's only through Jesus Christ and His blood that we approach the throne of God as we forgive others. **"Let us then approach the throne of grace with confidence, so that we may receive mercy and find grace to help us in our time of need" (Hebrews 4:16).**

When I was so hurt by my ex girlfriend and all that happened to me, the *last* thing I wanted to do was forgive her. After all, 95% of this was definitely her fault. I wasn't the one who cheated on her, *she* cheated on me. After I gave my life to Christ I was being taught these same things, and by faith I gave it to the Lord. Now, I'm not saying just once, but many times a day for a long time I kept giving it back to God because my flesh surely didn't want to forgive her of any of it. I am human, after all. It was over the course of time and giving it to God in faith that my feelings about her started to change to the point now where I honestly feel sorry for her. There's no anger or vengeful feelings, rather just compassion for someone who, as far as I know now, is still lost without Christ.

Un-forgiveness doesn't do anything to the person

who hurt you, but it surely affects you. You put your-self in bondage, and the other person is not affected at all necessarily. **"Do not take revenge, my friends, but leave room for God's wrath, for it is written: 'It is mine to avenge; I will repay,' says the Lord" (Romans 12:19)**. The Lord will chose when and how He shall judge that person, but it WILL come. **"It is a dreadful thing to fall into the hands of the living God" (Hebrews 10:31)**. Interestingly enough, I had talked to my ex girlfriend about 1 year after we broke up. I found out that she had gone through what she described as a very bad period of things happening to her since the spring time when she had asked me to marry her and I said goodbye. She didn't give me any specific details at all, but the way she said it sounded like the Lord started to discipline her for hurting me so badly. I may never know until I die, but God is faithful to bring justice to all. Whether in rewards or discipline, God is entirely fair and just ultimately.

A teaching you don't hear very often but is very true is found in **Matthew 18:21–35**, in **the parable of the un-merciful servant**. In this parable, Jesus describes a man (who could be any one of us) who owed an enormous amount of money to the king (who represents God). When brought before the king, he pleaded and begged for mercy. The king granted him mercy and cancelled his entire debt. I've heard it taught that this debt would be equivalent to $10 million dollars, maybe more as our society becomes wealthier. Whatever the amount, it was well beyond this person's ability to *ever* pay back the debt. The man, who was just forgiven this entire amount, saw a man after he left the king that owed him something along the lines of $5. Whatever the amount, it was nothing in comparison to what was owed to the king. This latter man begged and pleaded with the first man, who was forgiven much and was not given mercy or forgiveness. Instead, the man who was forgiven much had the man who owed him little thrown in prison until he could pay back the $5 debt. Other servants (people) saw both events and reported this back to the king. The king was furious. The king had him (the first man) brought before him and said he was a wicked servant. He asked why he didn't have mercy on this other man as the king had had on him. In his anger, the king turned him over to the *jailers* to be tortured until he could pay back his debt, which he could never do because it was so large. The jailers and torture represent demonic forces that God will allow in your life that will "torture" you until you forgive who ever has hurt you. Please do not misunderstand me. I know that there are things that are unspeakable to some of you that were done to you. You may be saying to me, "There is no way I could ever forgive them for what they did to me." I may not understand what you have been through, but I do understand that God's spiritual laws are never violated. God himself cannot ever violate a law He has put into motion, nor would He ever make an exception.

Your pain and healing (physical, spiritual, and emotional) can come through Christ as you forgive by faith and walk with the Lord over time. If you try to do it on your own it may very well consume you, as it has some in the past. Jesus knows how hard it is to let it go. It's your heart the Lord is always looking at. If in your heart you are trying your best to forgive and give it to the Lord, that's what matters most.

I was involved in a deliverance and healing ministry for several years in California. I realize most of the Body of Christ is either unaware or does not believe in some of the things I'm about to say; however, having witnessed these things firsthand, I can tell you they are completely real and true. Many say Christians cannot have demons based on several scriptural references. I understand their arguments for this. However, I also have witnessed Christians being delivered of demons firsthand who I know for a fact were born again believers. Satan uses what's commonly referred to as a "legal right" to oppress any person, saved or un-saved. A legal right means that the person has committed a sin, and it has gone un-confessed and un-repented to the Lord in a person's life. Once the person confesses the sin and asks for God's forgiveness, the legal right is broken. The demon or demons oppressing someone no longer have the legal right to be there any longer and must leave. This does not always mean they leave on their own even after a person confesses and repents. I've witnessed several demons who would not leave even after their legal right was removed. It was only after more time in dealing with the demon and taking authority over it that it finally leaves. I'm also not suggesting I am any great expert in this area, but I have seen enough to know a bit about this. It's like saying you believe in something of God. Until you actually experience it, it's hard to believe. My first times witnessing these things were very un-real. What I mean is, I believed the Bible and what it says about demons, and I read many books on deliverance. But until you actually witness it firsthand, you aren't "grounded" in what you have heard of or read about it. It's just like saying you believe the Lord will take care of you when you are broke. Until you are broke, you *really* don't believe it fully in your heart yet.

If you do not forgive someone, the scripture I spoke about earlier in **Matthew 18** where the king turns the unrepentant sinner over to the jailers is true. You MUST forgive if you want to be set free of this demonic bondage in your life. This will also help in restoring your relationship with the Lord, and help to bring healing to your own heart. When I speak with people these days, I can often pick out red flags in a conversation that there are areas of hurt and pain in someone's life that aren't dealt with yet. It's amazing to me just how many people around us, even Christians, are walking "wounded" people who need our prayers, support, and most importantly, Jesus Christ to heal them completely!

Just recently I prayed with someone who has been in a sexual struggle over pornography. This particular demon seems to be popping up everywhere in our society today with the propagation of the internet. No sooner had I started praying against the demon of pornography when it immediately manifested itself. This was after the Lord delivered me of my sexual addiction. I believe once you are an overcomer in a particular area, God anoints you even more-so in that area to drive out demonic powers. This person was and is a born again Christian by the way. It was the fastest manifestation of a demon I had ever seen.

Once while working on a construction job for a Christian friend back in California, we had a big misunderstanding about the job. Without going into details, he expected me to finish up something. I had a problem finishing the job before I left for a 4 day trip to New York and had planned on finishing up the job on my return. It was the best I could do. For my part, I miscalculated the amount of material I needed to finish the

Jeff Lacki

job. The job took longer on that last day before my trip so I had to leave. He had thought I was trying to go back on my word to complete the job, and it split our friendship at that point. I knew in my heart I didn't have any wrong intentions of not finishing, but it was my fault that I miscalculated the job. We went back and forth, and I was accused of being malicious in my intents. So we split over this. I felt that the Lord would deal with Him and I was in the right; after all, my intentions were not bad. I just made an honest mistake. I was also out several hundred dollars because of this since I didn't have a written contract. About 3 months went by, and the Lord really spoke to me about having to call him and apologize. I thought to myself, "Apologize? For what? I did everything above board and with integrity, and I lost money on the deal in the end. So what's there to apologize to HIM for, God?" That apparently didn't matter to God. He repeated the request to me over and over for several weeks. To be honest, I thought this man was quite mad at me still. I didn't want to call him for fear of getting reamed out on the phone. I decided to call him one day, and I apologized to him for what had happened. I was very sorry it all happened, plus I didn't want this thing to be between us any longer. This wasn't an easy thing to do either. It was the last thing I wanted to do, honestly! I had no idea how he was going to respond at all. I didn't see this friend very often, but it was still not a good thing. The amazing part was, the Lord had been dealing with Him about our situation as well, and had convicted him of several things. In the end, God was glorified and our friendship was restored. I never did get paid, but having things good between us again was worth far more than the money I had lost. In the end, financially speaking, God has more than multiplied some of the money I've lost in situations like these already! I could go on and on, but that's for another time.

In **Matthew 5:44**, the Sermon on the Mount, Jesus says, **"Love your enemies and pray for those who persecute you."** We are to pray for those who hurt us, not seek revenge as our fleshly human nature desires. **Proverbs 25:21–22** says, **"If your enemy is hungry, give him food to eat; if he is thirsty, give him water to drink. In doing this, you will heap burning coals on his head, and the LORD will reward you."** I can't say definitively what "heap burning coals on his head" means. I can say that this probably speaks to that person's conscience and pride, and will convict them ultimately.

Whatever the Lord means here, the message behind it is that love will overcome evil.

"Love never fails" (1Corinthians 13:8). This is not to say that you are to be someone's punching bag while they abuse you. Appropriate boundaries should be set in place if needed. But we are to love those who hate us and not seek revenge. I have heard many testimonies of bad people changing their hearts because love was shown to them when they weren't deserving of it. Often times it's just our day to day walk that others notice, and not necessarily what we say to them that leads them to Jesus Christ. If you are a true follower of Christ, your life will, for the most part, line up with His. **"By this all men will know that you are my disciples, if you love one another" (John 13:35).**

The Lord's Return is Near

For several years before I was saved, I was very much into prophesies, visions of the future, and all things paranormal and supernatural. I didn't study it as such, but I always watched television shows that were on. I was fascinated by it all. My limited belief and understanding of God was just enough to make me believe in many crazy theories and so called "prophesies and visions" of the future. As I've studied the book of Revelation, as well as Old Testament books such as Daniel and others in conjunction with things found in the New Testament about the end, my understanding of things has increased dramatically by God's Spirit.

I realize that many Christians out there either are not sure or do not think that the Lord's return will be in their lifetime. Many of my own Christian friends at times would say they weren't sure, or it will probably happen in 50 or 100 years from now. I have no doubt of their sincerity and love for Christ. I do know that Jesus spoke about the end in the Gospels. Indeed no man (or woman) can or will know the day or the hour of the Lord's return. However, I do believe that we know the times in which we live and can ascertain a reasonable time of His return (a ballpark figure). I'm not saying we should start trying to figure it out either. That should not be our focus.

Jesus Himself spoke about the end when asked by his disciples as to the signs of His return in **Matthew 24, Mark 13** and **Luke 21**. The signs truly are all around us even at this moment. The only portion of those scriptures that has clearly yet to be fulfilled is the preaching of the Gospel to every nation on the Earth. **"And this gospel of the kingdom will be preached in the whole world as a testimony to all nations, and then the end will come" (Matthew 24:14). "And the gospel must first be preached to all nations" (Mark 13:10).** Jesus also says, **"Even so, when you see these things happening, you know that the kingdom of God is near" (Luke 21:31)** and **"I tell you the truth, this generation will certainly not pass away until all these things have happened" (Luke 21:32)** again, **"Even so, when you see all these things, you know that it is near, right at the door" (Matthew 24:33).**

What things? All the things the Lord just spoke of prior to this. What generation? The generation who sees these things take place. This *is* our generation.

We are seeing this happen all around the globe at this time. Ministries in other countries are converting millions to Christ each year. The church is being persecuted like never before around the world, and even to a small degree in this country in the last couple years. It is certainly not to the point of death yet in this country, but the fact remains. The Lord said that anyone who would stand for Him would be persecuted. I believe this is about to happen in this country like never before. Even as persecution starts to intensify in this country, the power of the Holy Spirit will be poured out on all flesh to a greater and greater degree **"And afterward, I will pour out my Spirit on all people. Your sons and daughters will prophesy, your old men will dream dreams, your young men will see visions" (Joel 2:28).** The wicked will get much worse, but the miracles, signs, wonders, and everything else the Lord has for his end-time church will increase at the same time. One night during our prayer meeting I brought up the topic of the end found in **Matthew 24.** After we all discussed this, the Lord spoke this word to us:

My children, you would speak tonight and you would discuss the times in which you live.

You discuss my Word and what it would say of these times.

And it is wise that you would have this conversation.

It is good that you would discuss these things, for truly these are the days in which you live, and it does not help not to think about it.

It does not help to pretend that these times are not here or they will go away.

It does not help to think that it is a future generation that will live this life and go through these times.

For truly these are the times, and you must be prepared.

You must know the times in which you live and you must live them my children.

Let this night be as a teaching to you.

That as you discussed, it put a framework around your prayers and it directed your prayers.

For the kingdom moves forcefully forward for those who will take force and place their own hands upon it.

This is my desire:

That in your own hands you would hold the kingdom, that you yourselves would take force and you would help the kingdom to move forward and it is as easy as this evening, for truly it is your prayers that I desire.

It is your prayers from your heart that I see and that I respond to and that I work within.

It is in your prayers and humility that I cloak you in the mantle that you would do the work that I have given you to do and it is in requesting protection and the armor that I do indeed protect you, that though Satan would come against you, he would fail.

These are the times my children that you would seek after Me.

These are the times you would know Me.

These are the times you would stay close to Me, closer than you have before, because these are troublesome times for those who do not know Me, for those who are not close to Me.

These can be troublesome times my children, and yet they are times of my choosing.

They are times that have been spoken of and they are times that will be.

They are times that will come to pass; and you will stand before Me and they will be in your past.

You will see them as they happen and you will know that it is a time that is gone, for now your time is with Me.

And is this not your joy my children?

Is this not your hope?

Know that it is real.

Know that the home is prepared for you.

It awaits you already, and I myself have walked through the rooms, I have anointed the doorways, I have made the bed.

My children, the home is ready and it awaits you.

It is yours.

It is for you.

Let this be your faith as you live in these days.

Let it be your joy as you see the world about you and the changes that it will go through.

Do not be afraid.

The home awaits you my children.

These very words were spoken of this evening, and I say them now that you would know that I heard.

I say them now that you would know that it is true, and I say them now that you would be encouraged, that you would not grow faint, you would not be afraid, and that you would know my children that it is in your prayers that you will fight this battle.

I will use you in other ways, you will see things happen in your life, but it begins in prayer my children.

It begins in the anointing of the Holy Spirit, that you must carry within you and you must let flow through you for all the tasks that will be done for all the things in this time that will come to pass; and then, as you stand with Me you will look on these times and you will know that it was not of your own doing, it was only my Holy Spirit that allowed you to do these things.

It was my Holy Spirit for everything my children.

Persecution always brings revival as God's people stand for Him. The book of Acts is a great example of this. We are about to witness the greatest time in the history of the world, next to Jesus Christ living on Earth, in many of our lives. The Lord has repeatedly spoken to us in our prayer group telling us, "The time is shorter than you think."

My children, have I not talked with you in times past concerning your worship as you meet often to worship Me?

And I'm finding you faithful my children, in doing that; and what I am doing this evening in your midst is the beginning of a process, for you are tasting a little bit of the Glory that is forth-coming.

For as I prepare your tabernacles in the meeting place I remind you of what I did with Moses.

And did I not walk into his midst and we were face to face?

My children, I did that once and I desire to do it again in your midst as my children - as my creation.

This was my plan and this is what my purpose was.

And so I shall raise you to a new level.

You've never experienced high praise and worship my children, but as you do, as I prepare your vessels for that, for now you cannot tolerate that.

Your vessels are not prepared.

And so as you meet often and are faithful to worship, each time I shall prepare you, step by step for high praise and high worship.

And when this is done my children, I declare to you as the Lord your God, that the Glory will come into your midst and there shall be mighty acts that you shall see and you shall hear.

It is yours to partake in as you yield your tabernacle, your vessel, as a meeting place - and I will come down.

For it is not time yet for you to come to Me.

That day is shorter than you think, but before that

happens, I desire so longingly to come down into your midst.

So yield your vessels, yield this tabernacle that is being prepared for high praise and high worship, and I will be there in your midst - face to face.

For I am the same God as I walked with Moses, and I'm your God today.

Did not I declare that I wanted a whole bunch of people just like my servant Moses?

And I've been longingly searching for those.

My children, will you step forward this evening and the evenings to follow to yield your tabernacle for high praise and high worship?

And I declare to you, we will be face to face.

And again at another prayer meeting:

My children, I have been listening to the conversation, and it has been pleasant to my ears; for is it not my purpose from the foundation of the world to use you in these last days?

And so what I call you to this accountability my children, for the days are shorter than you think; and so what I am asking, that you would come and commit yourself for the tasks ahead, for they are many.

For there are much needs that need to be taken care of within my creation and within my children.

For I hear their cries and I have been looking for those who will come and minister to their needs - for you have already seen as you have read in the Bible what my Son did as He watched Me unfold before Him - and He saw what I desired to do in the lives of individuals.

He heard when I spoke to Him and He responded

in obedience - and is this not your requirement my children?

That you would place yourself in that relationship with Me so that I will show you things and I will tell you things of my Kingdom, for I am desiring that my Kingdom will come here on this Earth.

My Kingdom, from Heaven, will come nigh unto my people, my creation;

For that is why my Son went to Calvary and that is why I've called out those who will be sent ones to go and minister - in the days ahead that shall be your task if you so decide to do it, and as you move forward in this ministry to my people, to meet their needs,

I shall empower you.

Again I say my children, I shall empower you and let not fear and doubt and unbelief be a part of you, for it is not of Me, it is of Anti-Christ, and you must deal with these three, for they are very strong, and they will be in your life unless you come and guard yourself.

So again, come into accountability.

Put on the whole armor of God, and as you walk and you talk, I shall empower you, and signs and wonders shall follow those that believe, for I have said it in my Word and it is truthful.

And as you go in obedience you will see how truthful my Word is.

And the more you walk in obedience, the more you will see the truthfulness of my Word, for I cannot lie.

So I call you to step forward and step forward and step forward for the journey is there.

Jeff Lacki

The tasks are there waiting to be fulfilled.

Much needs that must be taken care of and I'm calling for laborers.

Will you step forward to this call?

If you do, be faithful and obedient, and again I say to you, I will empower you for the tasks ahead.

While this is both scary and exciting, we must not forget that **"Perfect Love cast out all fear" (1Timothy 4:7).** As the Lord said, fear, doubt, and unbelief need to be removed from our thinking and hearts. The times we live in are indeed becoming more and more fearful for those who aren't in Christ. Terrorism and natural disasters are on a major increase all around us. But for those of us in Christ, they are just more indications of the Lord's return. He called this the "birth pains." **"All these are the beginning of birth pains" (Matthew 24:8).** We need to be diligent to pray for each other and others who don't know the Lord. Satan will do his best to try and instill fear in our hearts, but we must remember that the Lord has overcome Satan. Fear should not be a part of our lives any longer. We need to trust Jesus in everything.

Faith

In **Hebrews 11:6**, the great faith chapter of the Bible, the Word of God says:

"And without faith it is impossible to please God, because anyone who comes to Him must believe that he exists and that he rewards those who earnestly seek him." In our day to day lives, it is very easy to get caught up in the flesh. We work, or attend school, or are housewives and many other things that our own life consists of. We have our own hopes, desires and dreams. We tend to work towards those things as life goes on. Even after you come to a belief in Christ and start walking with Him, we still fall into this routine of living our lives apart from the Lord.

At another prayer meeting, the Lord touched upon this very topic:

My children, is it revival that you desire?

Then come unto Me my children, come unto Me.

For surely it is the water of life that flows from Me.

Surely it is the water of revival that flows from Me.

And drink my children, drink of Me that you would be filled.

And you would thirst no longer, for only I will satisfy, only the water that flows from Me will satisfy, my children and will protect you and guide you in the days ahead.

Come unto Me I say.

Come unto Me for the times that are ahead and the days in which you live.

They are days that have been spoken of, they are days that have been prophesied, they are days that some have longed for, and yet others have dreaded.

These are the days my children.

It is the day of my living water, it is the days that will be fulfilled.

Drink of the water my children, you will not be dissatisfied.

Drink of the water and you will not be thirsty, for the water is my Spirit and you need my Spirit my children to live in this world and to live in this life as I would desire that you would be close to Me that I would guide you.

This is my desire my children, that you would drink and you would drink often.

That you would remember Me and that you would pray.

Let there be a time of prayer in your life and even beyond that, even as you would drive, even as you would work, even as you would shop, even as you would work in your yard, even as you would sit before the TV yet let your mind return to Me and drink my children, drink of Me.

Remember Me and do not forget Me.

Be with Me throughout your day.

Be with Me throughout your life, for it is my desire my children that you would not leave Me even as I never leave you.

Drink of Me my children, drink of Me, for I will fill you and I will give you the desires of your heart.

Jeff Lacki

Let your desire be of Me, for I will not disappoint, and I will only fill you with my water, the water of my Spirit.

Fear is the opposite of faith, and God richly rewards faith. Faith puts God's power into action. Faith expedites your prayers! Faith empowers you to do the things that God has laid out for you to do. Without faith it is *impossible* to please Him! What a statement. The world without God lives without faith. That is why they fear the things that we, as the true body of Christ, do not fear. As a born again Christian, you have *nothing* to fear. The One who created all things loves you. He watches over you at night. His angels keep charge over you in all your ways:

You will not fear the terror of night, nor the arrow that flies by day, nor the pestilence that stalks in the darkness, nor the plague that destroys at midday. A thousand may fall at your side, ten thousand at your right hand, but it will not come near you. You will only observe with your eyes and see the punishment of the wicked. If you make the Most High your dwelling–even the Lord, who is my refuge–then no harm will befall you, no disaster will come near your tent.

For He will command his angels concerning you to guard you in all your ways;

they will lift you up in their hands, so that you will not strike your foot against a stone. You will tread upon the lion and the cobra; you will trample the great lion and the serpent. "Because he loves me," says the Lord, "I will rescue him;

I will protect him, for he acknowledges my name. He will call upon me, and I will answer him;

I will be with him in trouble, I will deliver him and honor him.

With long life will I satisfy him and show him my salvation." Psalm 91:5–16

Many Christians I know or have met suffer from fear, doubt and unbelief. Many churches I've attended do as well. I'm referring more about Satan and his demons than anything else. Having been in the deliverance ministry and seen firsthand what demons do to people, both Christian and non-Christian, it breaks my heart that more Christians aren't outraged and angry over what he has done to people. Most of the problem, I've found, lies in the fact that 90% of Christians don't believe that demons are as prevalent as they truly are. Remember, our war is a *daily* war! Not an occasional one when we feel like fighting it. Satan's best weapon against the church (or one of them anyhow) is that he either doesn't exist, or demons and what they do to people are so rare it really isn't a big concern. Granted, we are always to be focused on the Lord, but our ministry must also include deliverance *as well as* preaching, teaching, healing, etc.

Fear, doubt and unbelief are some of Satan's strongest tools to keep us away from God. I admit there have been many times when fear and doubt were working to destroy my walk with the Lord, particularly where it related to finances and paying my bills. Doubt and unbelief have often been used against me, even as of yesterday, to make me believe that God does not have my best interests in mind over a spouse. Our greatest weapon against these things is the praise and worship of the Lord, no matter what we see in the natural. God is always working behind the scenes on our behalf.

My son, I speak truth to you, that in your life there are no accidents.

In your life, things do not just happen, for your life has been given to Me and I have taken it from you, that your life would proceed as I have planned and I have desired.

It is no accident that you would come to this place.

It is no accident that you would be here this evening, and it is no accident that you would meet in this room and you would kneel before the fire.

It is no accident my son, for you have heard Me speak that my love is as a consuming fire, and even so, my love is for you my son.

It is my love for you that never dies and is never quenched;

And if you would stand in front of a fire, though the world would be cold, yet you would warm your hands, and your face and your chest, they would be warm because they face the fire, and yet, even as your face grows warm, yet your back would grow cold because it is exposed to the world, it is exposed to the air.

The front of you would be warm and yet the back grows cold, and after a while you must turn that you would warm your back, and even the warmth that you gained in the front, you would lose it to the world.

Your hands would grow cold again, and so you would move, back and forth, always before the fire but always partly warmed and partly cold.

Partly satisfied and partly hungering for more.

And so it is my son, when the fire is outside; and

yet this evening my son I have moved the fire within your own heart that you would be warmed from the inside.

It is my love my son, it is my great love for you that will burn in your own heart and you will feel my presence, and you will know Me in a new way my son.

For truly I have waited for this time.

In all peoples lives I wait, that the door would open farther, that more room would be made, that my fire would grow larger.

And so it is my son, it is not that the fire was dead, it was not that it did not exist, but this evening I have burst it into flame within you my son.

Receive my love and know that it is beyond contentment that I would look upon you.

It is beyond the smile of my face, it is with great joy that I see you in your life my son.

It is with great joy that I would watch you live and I would watch you grow and I would watch you seek after Me.

It is with great joy my son, for this too, it is a consuming fire.

This too, it is the love of my heart.

This too my son, it is my love for you.

It is my love for you.

The evening this word was spoken to me was a cold winter evening in San Jose. My friends normally had prayer in the living room, but this night they decided to start the fireplace and have prayer in the backroom instead. I say this because it never ceases to amaze me how God directs our path and the path of others. This night, He directed the path of my friends and the evening to have prayer where there would be a fire going in the fireplace for me to kneel down and be prayed for apparently. Things like this truly have built my faith in Him. I share it that it would also build your faith as well.

As a software engineer, I often have to work on complex problems, some are more complex than others. I can get wrapped up in solving the issue and forgetting about eating lunch or taking a break. How much more often do I forget my Lord, Jesus Christ, while working? There are some days that are better than others. We have to remember that even though we live in the spirit with him, we also live right here on planet Earth in our bodies. **"And God raised us up with Christ and seated us with him in the heavenly realms in Christ Jesus" (Ephesians 2:6). "For our struggle is not against flesh and blood, but against the rulers, against the authorities, against the powers, of this dark world and against the spiritual forces of evil in the heavenly realms" (Ephesians 6:12)**. Remember, our flesh is *at war* with our spirit, and specifically the things of God. Ephesians 6:12 is also stating that our war is not against the people who irritate us or annoy us in our lives, but against Satan's kingdom in the spirit realm. The battle may be in the flesh, the mind, or both. Wrong thinking and demonic powers are everywhere today–just watch the news. The people themselves, if or when set free, are God's children as well. Paul says in **Romans 7:15, "I do not understand what I do. For what I want to do I do not do, but what I hate I do."** We are all guilty of doing what we know not to do or don't really want to do because we know it's wrong. The Bible, speaking of Moses, says, **"He chose to be mistreated along with the people of God rather**

than to enjoy the pleasures of sin for a short time" **(Hebrews 11:25).** Sin is pleasurable, no doubt, but in the end, leads to death**.** If sin were not pleasurable, we wouldn't have such a battle to stop it.

Even when we fail, God is right there, loving us, cheering us on, and calling to us to try again. Our job is to believe that He loves us. After all, He paid the ultimate price for us. I often think upon the Cross and His sacrifice. For as much as I've ever loved anyone, letting anyone beat me and do all to me that they did to Jesus far exceeds my limitations on love for anyone. This is primarily based on fear. Fear of pain, fear of hurt, fear of rejection, humiliation, and the list goes on and on. Most of us want to do what is right. We even want what is best for people, but very seldom will any one of us put ourselves on the line for another due to fear. In the same way, fear keeps us from attaining the things that God longs to give His children. We often desire to "control" our life and our future, as if that is ever entirely possible.

"Now listen, you who say, 'Today or tomorrow we will go to this or that city, spend a year there, carry on business and make money.' Why, you do not even know what will happen tomorrow. What is your life? You are a mist that appears for a little while and then vanishes. Instead, you ought to say, 'If it is the Lord's will, we will live and do this or that.' As it is, you boast and brag. All such boasting is evil. Anyone, then, who knows the good he ought to do and doesn't do it, sins" (James 4:13–17).

If God sent his one and only beloved son Jesus to die for you on the Cross, how much more does He desire to give you good things and not bad things? Don't get me wrong; I'm not preaching a gospel that is all happiness and no sorrow. The Lord also said, **"In this world you will have trouble. But take heart! I have overcome the world" (John 16:33).** There are seasons of joy and sadness in our life, whether we are believers or not. God desires to make us grow and use us for His kingdom plans. These plans include your reward for doing His will in your life, both here and after you die.

Faith is what pleases Him. Have you ever had someone not trust you? Maybe it was someone who knew you and still didn't trust you. It hurts more when you try to be an upright and honest person (saved or not). You've never lied to that person or cheated them in any way, and they still don't trust you. The worst mistrust of all comes in the covenant of marriage when one spouse cheats on another, lies to them, or does things that are dishonest. With that said, can you imagine how our Father, God, feels when we don't believe Him? He has done *everything* for you, given you life, good things (for most of us in this country), protected you, sent His only son Jesus to pay for *every* single sin you ever have or will commit, and you still don't trust Him? Many of you are saying, "Well I trust Him, but just not in the area of finances, or a spouse for myself, or over my disease or sickness." Whatever the area, I'm here to reassure you that He *does* care. He cares for you and your every need more than you can ever know. I know it doesn't seem like it at times. I've come to that place many times this last few years wondering, "God, do you *really* care about me as you say you do?" I sometimes hear Him laugh in my spirit. It's not a demeaning laugh, but a laugh of one that says I love you more than you can possibly know. I'm not just saying these words to you. I also have had my ups and downs over waiting for a wife to come into my own life. It also hasn't been easy being financially broke more than I've ever experienced while others around me prosper. This isn't just a couple years for me; it has been 7 years so far. Before I was saved, it was all my life minus the 3 years I was with my former girlfriend. But deep in my spirit, I know these things are true. Even now, I'm starting to see God's promises come to pass as my trials appear to be ending. Satan and his demons are the ones trying to tell us that God doesn't care, or somehow God is lying to us or "holding back." Just like in the Garden of Eden, Satan said to Eve, **"Did God really say" (Genesis 3:1)?** He tempted her with what she could gain from the apple. He tempted her with the eyes (the fruit looked good). He tempted her with what she could have by being like God (wisdom knowing good and evil). Satan hasn't changed much in the last 6,000 years.

This is a word the Lord brought to me one night after a prayer meeting in the parking lot of the church. I was asked by my friends to get on my knees. They would pray for me because I had shared just how low I was feeling that night (and many, many other times as well). I was at one of many points during these last few years when I could barely take the trials any longer. I didn't even want to go to this prayer meeting this evening because I was very depressed. As I knelt down on the pavement, the Lord spoke these words to me:

My son, in all of this world, in all of your life, I tell you the truth, there is one Jeff, there is only one you my son.
You are unique.
You are my son.

You are who I have made you to be and yet I speak truth to you, that in the very essence of man, in his very heart, all men are the same.

All people are the same my son; and so it is you would hear this evening that I would point out the beauty of this life and I would show the beauty of this world and I would ask if you would see it, and if you would see the beauty.

Do you not see it my son?

The beauty of this life, the beauty that is all around you, the beauty that I have given you my son.

Do you not see it and do you not cherish it?

Truly my son, everything you have, it is from my hands.

Everything you have you should cherish my son.

It is a gift from Me to you.

And in this time of trial my son, in this time of lack, do I not know your heart?

Do I not know your mind?

And is this not the essence of man?

You are unique and yet, you are completely the same my son, for all would feel the same.

All who would go through these circumstances, they would be the same my son.

And this is the time for you my son, it is the time of my choosing, that I would strengthen you and I would build you up, so that in the future in your life, as times would come, the trials would be upon you, yet you would stand firmly in faith, for you would remember the times my son, the times of testing, the times of lack, and yet you lived, and yet there was beauty my son.

Still there was beauty.

This is my desire:

That in all circumstances you would see the beauty of this world and you would know the beauty of your life, and you would walk hand in hand with Me my son.

For even for you, is this not your calling?

Is this not what I would have you do my son, that you would be with Me, that you would cherish each moment, and you would see the beauty, and it would be your joy my son, it would be your joy.

It is a time of testing my son.

Stand firm!

Be strong!

Love Me my son, do not turn away from Me.

Do not harden your heart towards Me.

It is a time for softening.

It is a time for brokenness.

It is a time for love my son, it is a time for love, for truly, I love you my son.

Never have I turned my back on you.

Never have I walked away from you.

Never have your prayers fallen to the ground.

I have heard each one.

They are collected in my hands my son.

Each one I have heard.

Each one I know, and each one my son, I will answer, in my way, in my time my son, in my beauty.

In my beauty in your life my son.

I once read in a vision the Lord gave someone about our prayers to heaven. It said that the Lord showed them a mailroom of sorts. Prayers that came with faith were marked "overnight" delivery, and the ones that came with little faith were marked "ground" delivery. In other words, prayers that are made in faith shall come to pass faster than those with little faith attached with the prayer. Even in the midst of impossible circumstances, we must have faith when we pray! I admit, there were many, many days I had little faith during my time of testing. God not only wants to test us, but He also allows us to see what's inside our own hearts during these trials. Once we see what's in our hearts, we can offer it back to Him and ask for forgiveness or healing or whatever needs to take place. We never fail a test; we just take it over and over until we pass it. I've learned to ask the Lord, "What are you trying to teach me through this circumstance?"

My son, in your life there are times when you would feel as though you are trapped.

You would feel the fence around you.

You would be entangled in the wire and you would feel like you are trapped and that the fence would keep you from stepping forward, stepping forward that you would pick up that which you desire to hold.

The fence would separate you.

The fence would entangle you.

The fence would keep you from that which is yours.

There are times my son that you would blame the fence on Me, that you would blame Me for the fence.

These are my words to you my son, that truly, you are my son and that truly, I would love you with an un-ending love, with a vast and great and deep love.

My son, you would not see the fence, but I tell you, it is a boundary on one side of you.

It is a boundary for your protection that would keep you from going where you should not go.

The fence is before you, but it is only on one side.

Turn around my son, for all about you, it is a big world, it is a big life and there is freedom for you.

There would be no fence to entangle you, for it is the direction that I have laid out before you that you would walk in it.

My son, do not over-analyze these words.

Do not contemplate them and look for a deeper meaning.

I tell you the truth, the meaning is plain.

I love you my son, I am making a way for you.

I am protecting you in your life.

Every day I would cause you to turn that you would see the life, that it spreads forth before you.

You would see the vastness of your life and the beauty of your life.

And there will be a time where you will look back and you will be grateful for the protection that I gave you for these times that I have brought you through.

You will not blame Me my son, you will praise Me.

This day is coming, I pray it will be now.

These are my prayers, that you would receive it now and know that is it true.

I protect you, I love you, even if you would not see it, even if you would not understand it.

Jeff Lacki

Still it is my heart for you and my love for you my son.

You are not trapped.

Keep on walking with Me.

You are not trapped.

You are not entangled.

Turn my son, as I will turn you.

You will see my son, the life you have, it is the life I have given you.

It is a beautiful life my son.

It is yours to live.

I give it to you my son,

I give it to you.

Finances

The Lord speaks a lot about finances throughout the Bible. In the Old and New Testaments, the Bible speaks of tithing and giving your first fruits to the Lord–not just financially, but also in time and material possessions. Before I was saved, I had a great job as a software engineer. I made lots of money and had lots to spend. I used to always say "I'm broke." It wasn't that I was broke. I just had bills that I needed to pay and didn't want to part with my hard earned money to pay them. It was my "carnal" nature. I was greedy and felt like I deserved even more. The Lord started teaching me about biblical financial responsibility. Let's face it; I didn't want to part with my money. I really didn't! After all, it was mine, I earned it, and not even God really had the right to tell me to give it away. As He started teaching me, I stepped out in faith and started painfully giving my 10% tithe to the church I attended. The Lord also tells us, **"Each man should give what he has decided in his heart to give, not reluctantly or under compulsion, for God loves a cheerful giver" (2Corinthians 9:7).**

I was definitely not so cheerful about parting with my money! It was only out of obedience to the Lord that I did so at first. Only after reflecting on His Word, and after a year or so had passed, did I realize my heart for giving had indeed changed. I became a very cheerful giver over the course of time, and hadn't realized it was happening. The Word says, **"For where your treasure is, there your heart will be also" (Matthew**

6:21). So in the course of my treasure going to God, my heart was growing towards Him as well. I didn't do anything to 'try' to make that happen. The Lord Himself has given me the faith and heart to give. I love giving now. To be very honest, money is a very nice thing to have, but it brings no true happiness in your life unless you can help others with it. It is a wonderful thing to have money to spare and spend on things. God does love to bless us with our desires and wants, as long as they are not sinful and are within reason. I do believe in prosperity teaching, but I assure you–if you haven't been faithful in little, God shall not make you faithful over much until you've proven yourself to Him. And that is done by Him and only Him, not by us. **"You have been faithful with a few things; I will put you in charge of many things" (Matthew 25:21). "Whoever can be trusted with very little can also be trusted with much, and whoever is dishonest with very little will also be dishonest with much. So if you have not been trustworthy in handling worldly wealth, who will trust you will true riches? And if you have not been trustworthy with someone else's property, who will give you property of your own?" (Luke 16:10–12).**

There are many people in the Body of Christ who teach a gospel of poverty. This means that in order to be truly Godly or spiritual, you must be poor like Jesus was. I'm not sure what Bible they are reading, but I see that Jesus came to give us life, and give it more abundantly to those who are in Christ. I see all over scripture that **"a sinner's wealth is stored up for the righteous" (Proverbs 13:22),** and **"to the man who pleases Him, He gives wisdom, honor and happiness, but to the wicked, He gives the task of storing**

and gathering up wealth only to hand it over to the one who pleases God" (Ecclesiastes 2:26). There are other examples as well.

The Gospel must be preached to all the world. How can it be preached unless we send those who are called? How can we send those who are called unless we, the Body of Christ, have the money to send them? The end-time harvest is practically upon us. The Church must have the finances to send them out. I believe that those who are righteous and faithful in their giving shall be the financiers of the end-time harvest.

Now don't get me wrong here. Some amount of that money that comes back to you is to bless you and take care of your own needs and desires. God only *requires* 10% as a starting point. Anything above that is called an offering. As I struggled for the last 4 years of under/unemployment from software engineering (as I did construction and handyman work), I always gave a minimum of 10%. Often times however, I gave far more when there was a particular need for the ministry/ministries that I support. You have to understand, I might only make $100 on a small job. I'd end up giving $10 or $20 back to the Lord. God has told me many times how that money shall come back to me a hundredfold. Have I seen it yet? No. You may say, "So how do you know its coming to you?" Well for one, God never lies. His Word (the Bible) is 100% true. Even when I don't understand the Word, if He wrote it, I know it is true. His mind is far bigger and smarter than my own puny, finite mind. I believe that this year, as I write this book, shall be the beginning of the greatest time of our lives, if not the history of the World. The desires of the Lord are starting to take place in greater and greater ways. I also believe and stand upon His promises to me that the finances shall be poured out into my own life, as well as the church. My job is to be faithful and re-seed that money back into His Kingdom so others can be saved by knowing Him as their Lord and Savior. This is at the heart of God, to save souls! As you do what God desires most, God then desires to bless you more and more. We often forget that it's all about God, *not us.*

An expression I heard recently said that you don't ever hear of someone laying on their deathbed saying, "I wish I had worked another day/week/month/year." No, they don't! How come? Because when you are in the most humble of circumstances, whether that is illness, sickness, or nearly dying, you realize what the most important things are in this life. If you haven't guessed yet, it's not money or things. It's relationship, whether that be to God, family, or friends, it is always relationship. Everyone knows you don't take a thing with you when you die. So why do so many spend so much effort and time acquiring possessions? Possessions are wonderful, but they are not everything and long-term, they do not bring true happiness.

Sex & Sexual Purity

You are probably asking, "Sex?" What's this about, especially in a Christian book? Sex was, after all, created by God for our pleasure and enjoyment, but only within the confines of a covenant marriage relationship. I added this chapter due to the fact that I've been single for such a long time. Waiting for the fulfillment of sex and other things in a marriage that the Lord shall give to me soon hasn't been easy, to say the least. It's also an area that I should give some testimony, encouragement, and some teaching. I'm unfortunately a man who has been there and understands the pain, heartache and struggle that comes with singleness. They say singleness is a gift of God. I understand why this is said. You are very free to go where God would send you and do what God would ask you to do without any other commitments. At the same time, it says in **Genesis 2:18, "It is not good for the man to be alone, I will make a helper suitable for him."** While this passage indeed speaks of men more than women, it is still very true that it speaks to women as well. It is not good for any of us to be alone, whether married or not. We all need fellowship and friendships in our lives to remain healthy. This verse also speaks to most of us at least needing a spouse or helpmate in our lives. Even some forms of torture include isolation. Why? Because God did not create any of us to be alone. It is also where Satan can really work against us in our mind and emotions, in isolation.

Even as I write this book, my struggle to do what

God commands is still a daily and sometimes hourly battle over lust, singleness and sex. Satan knows that he has no part in me (for the most part) except where it comes to my singleness and needs for a spouse. I have never even tried drugs (except as they were ever prescribed to me) and I rarely drink alcohol, but my natural desire for a woman has been the only part of my life Satan continues to use against me. I also realize this won't end after I'm married. It is the largest battle in my walk with the Lord, so much so that there have been many, many times where I've wanted to turn my back on the Lord and go have "fun" for a while. It's certainly not for lack of opportunity in today's perverse society. After all, it sure seems like the rest of the world is doing so, and sadly enough, quite a few Christian brothers and sisters are as well. Sometimes it has caused me such heartache waiting on the Lord that I've told God to kill me. I couldn't take the struggle within myself to do what I know is right, and yet fall so far short of it. I've even told the Lord how much I hate the sexual drive to begin with because it makes us say and do stupid and sinful things at times.

The Lord talks about "adulterous Israel" many times in the Bible. God was constantly trying to bless and love Israel. For periods of time they were obedient and loved the Lord with all their heart, and time and time again they fell away from God into "spiritual adultery." They chased after their own idols instead of the Lord Himself. We are the same. We say we love God, but we still have "idols" setup in our hearts that are not of God or for God. God's entire design of us (the Body of Christ) and Himself is shown by the Body of Christ being made into the Bride of Christ someday soon. The male and female relationship in marriage is

Jeff Lacki

also a portrait here on Earth of the heavenly way Jesus is the bridegroom and we are the bride. For many men, it can kind of freak us out a little bit. It is because we are men, and Jesus is a man from a human perspective. Loving Jesus for me was hard at first because my mind was so in the gutter from the filth of the world before Jesus started cleansing me. As a man has intercourse with his wife, his seed is implanted in her body. So it is when we give our hearts to Jesus and ask for his forgiveness He gives us his Holy Spirit within our body, in the spirit realm of course. At that very moment, we pass from death to eternal life. **"No one who is born of God will continue to sin, because God's seed remains in him; he cannot go on sinning, because he has been born of God" (1John 3:9).** The seed here is the Holy Spirit, given as a deposit on the day you were born again. There is much more that can be said about this verse, but I wont elaborate on those parts. My example of God's seed is sufficient for what I'm describing here.

The Word also says, **"and the two will become one flesh.' So they are no longer two, but one" (Mark 10:8).** In God's eyes, when you consummate the marriage by having sex, you become one flesh. Yes, you are still 2 individuals, but God also sees you both as one. When you have sex, you become "soul tied" with the person you are having sex with. If you have sex with others–whether in or outside marriage–you are becoming one flesh in the spirit with them as well. It's also robbing you of your own soul as you give yourself away to others, unless it is to your spouse within the marriage covenant. The Lord can break the soul ties created when we sin. **Hebrews 12:4** says, **"For the Word of God is sharper than any two-edged sword, even**

dividing the soul and spirit." What man has joined, God *can* separate through repentance and asking Him to separate you. This is not to say that we should go on sinning by having pre-marital sex or continue in adultery! Many single "Christians" continue in this sinful behavior as an excuse that they cannot wait or overcome their desire. This is true; *they* can't. But God can through His Holy Spirit. He can help them in their lives if they continually ask for it and *willfully* chose not to sin in this manner. I admit that there have been far too many times I wanted to just have sex because the drive was more than I could bear. I thank God that thus far I have not given into that temptation. I often think of my future wife and how I'd feel if she does that before we marry. You really are cheating your future spouse and yourself of a great gift that God will bless you with if you remain pure. Consider the following scriptures concerning sexual immorality:

"But among you there must not be even a hint of sexual immorality, or of any kind of impurity, or of greed, because these are improper for God's holy people" (Ephesians 5:3).

"For of this you can be sure: No immoral, impure or greedy person–such a man is an idolater–has any inheritance in the kingdom of Christ and of God" (Ephesians 5:5).

"The body is not meant for sexual immorality, but for the Lord, and the Lord for the body" (1Corinthians 6:13).

"Flee from sexual immorality. All other sins a man commits are outside his body, but he who sins sexually sins against his own body. Do you not know that your body is a temple of the Holy Spirit, who is in you, whom you have received from God?

Jeff Lacki

You are not your own; you were bought at a price. Therefore honor God with your body" (1Corinthians 6:18–20).

Many men and women think that anything other than intercourse is ok to do, such as oral sex, masturbation and other things. I assure you, it is not. It's all sin. **Ephesians 5:3** clearly shows that without question. Just because we cannot hold back our natural desires for sin does not in any way, shape, or form mean that God makes exceptions and it's ok to sin sexually. Yes, God does understand our sinful nature, but He also expects us to try to fight against evil and sin in our lives. He takes it very seriously, even warning us of consequences that come from such sins. He says both in **Leviticus 11:44** and **Leviticus 11:45, "Therefore be holy because I am holy."** God *does expect* holiness from us and it IS possible only by His Spirit.

Now, I am not judging singles who have slipped in these areas. God knows your heart and He knows just how much you can bear. I have gotten into many, many sexual conversations with women who I met online over the past few years. I was trying to fill the loneliness and emptiness I was feeling. Online addiction is very difficult to break. I always confessed my sins to my accountability partners and God, of course. They prayed with me each and every time, in love, not condemnation. The truth is, sex is the one thing that God himself cannot fulfill for us. He created the sexes for the physical aspects of a relationship as well as companionship and many other things. If you have fallen in these areas, I encourage you to repent each and every time. Constantly pray and plead with the Lord to deliver you and help you. Ask other brothers or sisters who are trustworthy in the Lord to stand in prayer with you daily as you try to overcome this demonic addiction. This *is* a Satanic bondage. Whether you believe a Christian can have a demon or not, it only comes from *one* place–hell! Also remember, God requires obedience before blessings will come forth. These things are truly demonic bondages that only the Lord can help deliver you from. **"Submit yourselves, then, to God. Resist the devil, and he will flee from you" (James 4:7).** God's arms are always open to receive you and wash you clean in the blood of Jesus. If Satan tries to remind you of your sins, just rebuke him and claim God's Word over you. You are washed clean by the blood. **"Therefore, there is now no condemnation for those who are in Christ Jesus" (Romans 8:1).** Remember, Jesus gave his entire life for you! He knew you before you were born. He's always there ready to receive you if you will give yourself back to Him. God already saw every sin you'd commit before you were ever born. Still, He has given you a free will to *choose* to do right and not wrong! If you hear God's voice speaking to you, do not harden your heart. Remember, God cannot work with hard clay as He can with clay that is still malleable and soft, which is your heart.

I also need to add that many forms of sexual problems and issues are demonic bondages that you may need to be delivered from specifically. What I mean is, pray about finding a group of people involved in a deliverance ministry that can help you or even deliver you by God's power. It's an area that I cannot go into more detail with in this book, but there are many books on deliverance out there. I encourage you to pick one up and find out more. Definitely pray about it! You *can be* set free!

My deepest struggle has been what I prefer to

say as "solo sex." Masturbation is a word I really hate, probably due to the shame that Satan tries to put on me about my struggle in this area all of my life. I know many Christian men and women struggle in this area, let alone non-believers. Non-believers don't think it is a sin, and sadly many Christians do not think it is either. The fact is, Jesus didn't do this behavior. He *is* and *was* a Holy person, sinless in all His ways. He was tempted as we are, yet without sin. Are you tempted to masturbate? It is most certainly a sin and very likely tied to lust, which most of us struggle with from time to time in our lives, married or not. Submit to God, resist Satan, and it will flee from you. You must constantly try to resist, but you must also always submit yourself to the Lord first.

When I was in high school, I attended an all-boys Catholic school in Chicago. Guys were constantly joking about the subject, so much so that I became curious and started at the age of 16. I suppose that's old compared to some young people these days, and with the perversity that is in our world. When I gave my life to the Lord in 1998, I realized that those behaviors were not right as I came to know Him more and more. It was a struggle, but it wasn't until 3 years after being saved that it really became a much larger issue, which I have dealt with even through the writing of this book. It was so bad that I decided to go on a 21 day fast, 1 meal a day to break the bondage. After 21 days, the Lord told me to go 40 days, which I reluctantly did because the fast was so hard. You think fasting 1 meal a day isn't too big of a deal, but it is. I can't imagine a full (no food) 40 day fast! I noticed that the spirit of lust I was dealing with was very much weakened during my fast, though not immediately. One great thing about fasting for the Lord is that you can feel His presence much more than when you aren't fasting, at least for me. He comes in the middle of me watching television, or other odd activities out of the blue.

After my fast was over, the same behaviors came back almost immediately. I decided 2 months later to do a 21 day fast (1 meal a day) to start my year off for the Lord on the right foot. I was giving my "first fruits" to Him, as it were. I also did it to continue to help break this sexual bondage. I was desperate for deliverance over this for such a long period of time that I did these 2 fasts. 1 year later, in January 2005, I did the same thing. I fasted another 21 days at the beginning of the year to help break the bondage of sexual addiction and lust, and to give my year to the Lord. Still I was not delivered from this bondage.

The last 3.5 years have been the bulk of the bondage in my life. The way it started was this: I had become unemployed and needed extra income to help pay the mortgage on the house. I took in a Christian man who went to our church. Shortly afterwards, he also lost his job. I let him stay because that was the right thing to do. I would go out to the few handyman jobs I had and come home after a long day. My new roommate was very often still sitting on the couch. He would be watching television in his robe at 3pm or 5pm, depending on when I was done. I'm a person who likes my privacy, and so I would go into my home office and spend a lot of time online chatting with women since the living room was taken over by him. This is where my problem took serious root. After another 5 months of this going on, I finally asked him to leave. After that day I swore I would never take in another roommate, Christian or not, unless I was married to her. My roommate was depressed and had other issues going on. I strongly believe these "spiritual" elements in my home led me down the wrong path. I was weak at that time as well, even though I knew better. A spirit of depression was definitely in the house; only God knows what else was brought in.

Men are wired so differently than women are, especially in the area of visual stimulation. This is why most men vs. women struggle with pornography. There are other reasons as well that I won't mention here. The age in which we live is constantly and persistently pushing sexual images down our throats. It's telling us that sex is natural and not to hold back your desires, whatever they are and however perverse they seem to be. One time in particular, when I was deeply struggling over this and asking God question after question about why He made me with this desire, He spoke this word to me:

My son, many times in your life you would sit before Me and you would speak to Me, and always I am before you my son, and always I would hear, and I would hear your questions.

"Why is this that way?"

"Why have you made me this way?"

And yet, there is no relief and there is no joy.

"Why are things as they are? For truly you would hold them in your hands and truly you would control all things."

You would quote the Word to Me and you would ask why?

My son, I have enjoyed these times, even as you would question, I would watch your mind work, it is very active my son.

Truly it is a gift that I have given you when it is applied in the way that I would have it be used.

My son, the times are changing, the times are changing, for even as you were saved, you would take your hands and you would measure out the ground and you would lay your tent and you would drive the stakes - with your own hand my son, it is a tent of your making.

Yet I would see more my son and I would take my hands, and my hands are larger than your own my son, and I would lay out the ground and I would plot the area for your tent, and so it is, your tent would stretch, and so it is, I would drive the stakes my son.

It is a larger ground, a larger area than you would think and larger than you would know.

My son, is it worth it?

That your tent would stretch and that you would stretch?

That there would be more of you, there would be more of Me in you?

Is it worth it my son that I would use you for greater things?

And is it not my way my son that I would know the end, and yet you are living it out and still do not see it and still do not know?

Are these not questions my son that I could ask of you, and yet, I do not ask my son, for I encourage you and I bless you and I tell you, greater things are ahead of you my son, greater days are ahead of you, for truly, I have laid the plan for your tent my son.

Truly, I have driven the stakes, and what I have driven, they cannot be pulled out my son, they can-

not be moved, and I am stretching you, that you would grow into this area, that you will grow into your calling that I have placed upon you.

It is all for good my son, it is all for joy.

It is for you, and it is for Me my son.

Have faith!

Be encouraged!

Stand tall my son!

For truly, I am doing a great thing in your life, if you would see it.

I am doing a great thing in your life, if you would know it.

It is a great thing my son,

It is a great thing.

I would strongly encourage women, especially Christian women reading this, to really understand what men go through by how you dress. Men are very visual. It's why so many men struggle over pornography. Most women do not–why? Because they aren't as visually stimulated as men are in that area. It has caused me and many other Christian men I know much heartache. It's from being single and trying to maintain our sexual purity while waiting for a spouse. I'm not sure if this example fits, but if men were able to somehow fulfill part of your desire for a man outside a relationship when you were around them, and yet it wasn't fully fulfilled because you aren't married, how would you feel? You would feel frustrated, angry, or look to complete that need apart from Gods plan for your life in an unhealthy or ungodly way. So please do us men a favor and save inappropriate dress for your marriage and within the home, where possible. Church is definitely not a place to dress up entirely. Even as women like how men look in suits, so also men are attracted to women in dresses on Sunday mornings. My personal opinion is that dressing down, but not too far down, on Sunday mornings for church is a good thing. Ultimately, God knows your heart towards Him and your motives. In this day and age when those images are everywhere around us, the last thing we men need is to see them at church on Sundays. If you are married, do your husband a favor and dress up at home. I would encourage men and women to read books on the opposite sex and find out what things both sexes enjoy and love the most. I would hope and pray for every marriage out there in all these areas. I pray that you would be enjoying the natural sexual desires that God has given each of us, and you are freely able to do within the confines of your marriage under biblical principles. After all, some of us aren't able to enjoy that freedom yet.

I remember during my rebellious period when I was so deeply hurt and looking for a woman in my life, Satan was putting thoughts in my head that I had never had before. Thoughts that I cannot even mention here–all kinds of perversions that I knew were wrong. I thank God I knew better and didn't even consider those thoughts:

"When tempted, no one should say 'God is tempting me.; For God cannot be tempted by evil, nor does he tempt anyone; but each one is tempted when, by his own evil desire, he is dragged away and enticed. Then, after desire has conceived, it gives birth to sin; and sin, when it is full grown, gives birth to death" (James 1:13–15).

At that time I didn't understand that they weren't really *my* thoughts. They were being sent to me from Hell, literally. If you are having thoughts and they are

Jeff Lacki

really bothering you, pray that Jesus covers your mind in the blood of Jesus. Always pray for the full armor of God upon you as well. **"Put on the full armor of God so that you can take your stand against the devil's schemes" (Ephesians 6:11).** The Lord wants to give you the heart and mind of Christ. Even thoughts against the Lord can occur in your head, and you may be wondering what's going on. I've had many occasions, especially when I was a new believer, when curse words would pop into my head towards the Lord over and over. I knew it wasn't what I really was thinking, but before I knew these things I felt very ashamed and guilty. Looking back, it was Satan trying to put those things on me by putting those bad things into my head over and over. We have to remember that Satan has had approximately 6,000 years to learn how humans think and feel. He can hear our conversations, but he can never know our thoughts or prayers in our mind (unless he put a thought there to begin with). Satan is always working in our minds and emotions to cause us to fall. If we fall, the sins we commit only lead toward greater and deeper sins. In the process, your heart will grow colder and colder towards the things of God and God Himself.

I've often wondered why alcohol and drugs were such a problem and addiction for so many people. The Lord has really shown me that just because I don't have a problem with it doesn't mean the issues aren't very real for those who suffer with those addictions. The same is true with homosexuality, bi-sexuality and lesbianism, or any other sin in your life. I've come to believe that no matter who you are, there's at least one thing in your life that Satan has the potential to use against you as you try to walk with the Lord.

For me, it's my natural desire for a woman; for others, it's drugs, alcohol, etc. We all need to walk in humility and honesty before the Lord and others. **James 5:16 says, "Therefore confess your sins to each other and pray for each other so that you may be healed."** We should confess our sins, yes, but only to those who we know are Godly men and women who will pray with us and for us. **"A cord of three strands is not quickly broken" (Ecclesiastes 4:12).** It's important to be in fellowship with other believers. Remember, we are in a spiritual battle daily!

Even as I have been writing this book, the Lord has delivered me from a spirit that has brought so much heartache and struggle in my life. Last week, as I was crying out to him for deliverance of this bondage, I started having thoughts of a time when I was around 8 years old at my grandparents' house. I was in bed next to my grandfather trying to fall asleep. He was fast asleep. For hours I was being tormented with sexual thoughts of women. I remember thinking, "Where are these coming from?" I do some of my best praying in the shower, and it was in the shower that the Lord revealed to me the name of the spirit that came when I was 8 years old. This spirit was giving me the bulk of the grief I have been experiencing now for years. Its name was "fantasy." It was like a light-bulb went off in my head. So I prayed against it immediately for several minutes, commanding it to leave me in Jesus' name and repenting for the sin of fantasy in my life. About 30 minutes later as I went to bed and was praying, I started coughing and coughing for about 10 minutes. I thought I was getting sick, like most people are lately with the flu season upon us. I realized the next day that the oppression was, for the most part, gone.

I wasn't sick either, nor did I become sick. That spirit had left me! You have to realize, I had been oppressed for years by this thing. I was in a deliverance and healing ministry for several years, and have learned much about demons and deliverance. I have seen some things that I cannot share here due to the unbelief of it all by many. I found it very hard to believe as I experienced it before my very eyes as well. What I will say is, even in the midst of ministering to others and having been prayed for by our deliverance group, I still had a spirit that apparently was there since I was 8 years old. I continued to struggle with this sexual addiction, but it was severely weakened after this.

Again, if you don't agree with me here, that's ok. I'm just sharing with you the story as it unfolded in my own life. I know of many Christians and pastors who do not agree that Christians can have demons. We are all God's children still, and it is the Gospel we need to stay focused on. Since then, nearly 3 weeks ago now, I've found a new strength come over me in that area. I'm not perfect yet, as it's still a habit that has been going on in my life for many years. But the compulsion to act upon it has significantly decreased. God is making me into an overcomer in that area. I'm very grateful, as always, for His work in my life and on the Cross!

Other Testimonies

During my 7 years as a Christian, I have never looked back and put on paper what God has done in my life. I added this chapter because there were so many smaller things the Lord did, and I didn't want to overlook them or leave them out of this book. After all, when will I ever write another autobiography? I won't say never, but you never know. It says in **John 21:25, "Jesus did many other things as well. If every one of them were written down, I suppose that even the whole world would not have room for the books that would be written."** For myself, there were so many things that the Lord did, both small and large. If I had a better memory and much more space, I suppose I too could write many more pages of what the Lord has done. I will attempt to add just a few of the more significant ones here that I can recall in no particular order.

Once I was saved back in 1998 I started praying for each of my family members daily. About 3 years after I was saved, my mom, dad and brother had the opportunity to come to California. They were willing to be baptized all at once by my good friend Pastor Varkey. More amazingly than that, the night before the baptism, they came to a prayer meeting with me. The Lord spoke to each of them prophetically as well. We were all in tears for the things the Lord spoke. The words to each of them were entirely true. Each of them re-dedicated their lives to Christ that evening. The Lord told my brother He was setting him free from many things that evening. He told my brother that Satan took him captive 12 years earlier to lead him away from the Lord. I had no idea what happened 12 years ago, but my brother told me later that was when his alcoholism started. My brother had struggled with alcohol for years. After his trip, he noticed it wasn't a problem any longer. My brother also had struggled with severe anxiety attacks, and has since noticed they are very minor compared to what they were. I believe he is still in an on-going process of being delivered. Praise the Lord!

I was also praying a lot for a cousin of mine during this time. It was about 4 years after I became saved and had been praying for her that she turned her life to the Lord as well.

I had had what's called a plantar wart on the bottom of my big toe for the first time back in 1992. They can be quite painful, so I saw the doctor. He removed it with laser surgery, which was also very painful because they have to do what's called a "nerve block" on the toe beforehand. About 1 year went by and it was back. I had it removed again by laser surgery. This went on year after year on the same toe for 9 or so years and 7 surgeries. I had had my last surgery just before getting saved. About 1 year later it started to return. I told the Lord that I believed in healing and that I had done everything I knew to do to get rid of it by natural means. Now I was trusting Him to heal me for good. Another year went by, and the bottom of my toe became what I jokingly say as "leprous" with this wart that was now spreading. In fact, it started to spread to my other toe as well. It concerned me, but I tried to stay focused on God's power to do all things and trust in Him. Besides, I had many other things on my mind that I was praying for at the time. I anointed the toes with oil, and prayed for them as often as I remembered to for God's healing. At some point, I became so busy that I had forgotten about the toe and to even pray. Several months had gone by when I realized I hadn't checked out the toes to see how they were doing. To my extreme amazement, both toes were completely healed! I should say that they were never too painful to begin with typically, so I never noticed the pain go away. You can see the scars from the previous surgery, but the skin itself is completely normal. Another great testimony of God's amazing power!

Before I gave my life to Christ, I was one of the "sickest" healthy people around. My mom and I joked about that a lot because I was always coming down with the flu or a cold. I was easily sick about 5 times a year. My doctor's file was more than an inch thick in the 8 years I had been in California. After I gave my life to Christ, I noticed I didn't get sick any longer. In fact, I think in the past 7 years I've only had the flu twice, and both times it was quite bad, but no minor colds or flues since. There have been many other times when a sore throat or cold would start to come on me. I would rebuke the illness in Jesus name and get better within hours. God's Word is true! **Isaiah 53:5** says, **"But he was pierced for our transgressions, he was crushed for our iniquities; the punishment that brought us peace was upon him, and by his wounds we are healed." "Otherwise they might see with their eyes, hear with their ears, understand with their hearts and turn, and I would heal them" (Matthew 12:15)**. You may remember **Isaiah 53:5** being displayed at the beginning of Mel Gibson's movie **"The Passion."** As I speak about later in the chapter "It is Finished," Jesus' work on the Cross 2,000 years ago completed our healing by what He suffered for us. Jesus didn't suffer just for our physical bodies, but also our emotional healing, deliverance, and all things that are good from the Lord. It's all available to each of us if we have faith and do not let go, no matter what things appear to be in the natural. God is longing for people who will take Him at His Word and believe Him!

At some point after I lost my last software position and was trying to make ends meet, I helped a friend of mine install a 220V outlet for her new washer and dryer. I did it for free because she asked me to, and I wasn't doing much of anything else at that time. This was before my handyman business. A couple weeks after I was done, I went to a party with her and other friends. Her mother came up to me and handed me a check for $500 for helping her daughter out. This was completely out of the blue. She thanked me for helping her daughter. She knew that I was in rough times, financially, so she gave me the money. I was quite thankful, as always!

Before I lost my job, I was making quite a bit of money. It was so much that I was able to give a lot away to mission work and the church. I would also pay for meals for nearly everyone I was out with. I did it because most of the people I knew were making less than I was. I really enjoy giving now that I really know the Lord. After I lost my job, I started to notice just how often other people fed me after our Bible studies and other such meetings, or even just took me out to eat for free. It says in **Luke 6:38, "Give, and it will be given to you. A good measure, pressed down, shaken together and running over, will be poured into your lap. For with the measure you use, it will be measured to you."** Over and over, God continues to prove His Word to me.

At one of many other low spots in my finances, a relative sent me another $500 unexpectedly. It may seem like money was just falling from heaven for several of these testimonies, but there were just a few times when money came as a gift out of the blue. Primarily I had to work for it, the little that I did work.

Other Prophetic Words

I added this chapter because there were some other prophetic words that I felt were significant to encourage you, the reader, and I didn't have a specific place to put them prior in the book. I hope they encourage and bless you as they have me!

As I was growing in the Lord, my friends started giving me books to read. Some of the books were of people the Lord had actually taken to Heaven and shown around. I started praying to see Jesus and go to Heaven as well. I don't know if this word is forever, but for now, this is what the Lord told me:

My son, if I were to take you my son, to the glory that you would open your eyes and you would see.

If I were to take you my son, to the rising sun, you would be in the light and you would see the glory about you, then you would know my son and you would understand.

Yet I tell you, it is for my glory, that though not seen, though not understanding, yet there is faith and yet there is love.

It is for my glory my son, that you would not see Me and yet you love Me.

That you would not know Me and yet, your heart is for Me my son.

It is for my glory, and I speak truth to you:

It has been prayed that I would stretch forth my hand, that I would grab a hold of your job...of your finances...and I would draw them to you.

But I have a higher target my son.

I have a higher target than these things.

Is it not your heart my son?

Is it not you yourself?

And know now that my hand is upon you, and firmly I have grasped you, that you would not depart from Me... that I would hold you to my bosom...I would bring you to my heart and you would know Me my son.

I will never let loose of you.

You are a chosen one for Me my son.

You are a child in my own arms, and I will protect you.

My love showers upon you.

Tears of joy fall upon you that I would bless you and I would anoint you.

Though you would not see Me, yet I love you my son.

Though still you would not know Me, yet I know you.

I have set a higher target my son.

I will make the way.

Stay close to Me, do not lose faith, do not lose heart, and know that even as you do, yet my hand is still upon you.

Yet still I do not let loose of you.

Still you are my son.

Still you are my chosen one.

I will make the way my son.

Do what is placed before you.

These are my words to you my son, these are my words.

This word came during a time that I was asking God to

speed things up in my life. I had seen how incomplete I was and wanted to know more and be more:

My son, with your own eyes you would look upon this world and you would see its beauty and its greatness.

For through all my creation, all that your eyes would behold, there is nothing that is un-finished.

There is nothing that I began that I did not complete.

All things my son, are complete.

All things are perfect.

And in your eyes you would see the sky, you would know that it is true.

In your eyes you would see the mountains and you would know their beauty, and they are complete my son, they were complete by my hand.

Even as you would look upon the young tree, though it is still short in your eyes, yet you would know, that it too is perfect and that in time it will grow, and though now you would look down upon it, yet in the future you will stand under its branches and it will shade you from the sun.

It will stand tall before you, and it is perfect my son.

It is complete, though now you would look upon it and it is young, yet in the future you will look at it and it is old and it is tall.

And so it is that in your life, in your prayers my son, you would ask that you too would grow, that you too would be complete.

You would ask that the process would be sped up, that though for many years the tree would grow, that your desire would be to see it in its fullness as it is complete.

It is your desire that you would look upon yourself in the same way my son, and so it is, I have answered your own prayers my son.

So it is that I would bring you to a place that would take you a long time my son, to achieve the things that you achieve, to have the faith that you would have to understand Me, for even now there is more to Me than you would know.

There's more than you can understand.

It is a process my son, it is a growth, and yet still I say, "It is complete my son."

For this day in your life, it is complete for where I would desire you to be, and tomorrow my son, though you would see the lacking and though you would desire more, I say to you, you are complete my son, because you are in Me and I would make you complete.

These are my words my son, that you would be satisfied.

That your desire for Me would be above all and that you would never be satisfied in your desire for Me, that in the things of this world, those things that I would give you, the things for this day, they are enough for you my son.

Let your joy be complete, and truly I say to you, let your faith rise up.

Let your faith rise up my son, for it brings joy to my heart.

It is a wonderful thing in my eyes, even as you would look upon the tree and you would see it as complete, you would admire its beauty, so it is as

I would look upon you and I see you are complete and I admire your beauty my son, I admire your beauty.

Another time when Pastor Varkey was in town, I was asked to pray for him. I prayed for his church, family, and their finances as I often do. To my surprise, the Lord then spoke to me:

My son, you would lift your voice to Me.

You would pray my son and you would pray unto Me.

I speak these words to you now that your faith would grow in you, and that you would know that there is another who has prayed for you.

There is another who has spoken on your behalf.

There is another who has blessed.

It is I myself my son, for truly I would sit at the right hand of the Father.

Truly I would speak your name that you would hear that truly you are my blessed son, that you are the one I love.

For you my son, I have asked for blessings, and so it is that you have lifted your voice to pray for another that you have been praying my son, and so it is I have heard and I have prayed for you.

Let this be your faith, I have prayed for you my son.

What I pray, it shall be.

Nothing can stop the things that I have desired.

Nothing will stop what I have spoken.

It is spoken my son.

It shall be.

Let this be your faith.

My son, in this world there is great noise, and in this world there is turmoil.

In this world, my son, where you would live there is hardship and there is struggle.

So it is my son that you are in the world, but you are not of this world, for you have seen a higher place and you have had truth spoken to you.

You have felt my touch, my son, and you would know that you are no longer of this world, though you once were, for I have changed you my son - that your thoughts would go beyond this world, and your motives would go beyond that of even your own heart, that they would be as my motives, for truly, you would be as my own heart my son; and I tell you now that though there is much in this world that would distract you and there is much in this world that would weigh heavily upon you, yet my son, the peace is a moment away for you, and the peace is but a few words away for you my son, that as you would leave this world, and in your prayers my son, you would seek Me, more than the words you would speak my son - in the surrendering of your heart - in the stillness of your heart, my son.

It is then that you are far from this world, and the cares of this world - they seem so small my son, for truly they are behind you.

My son, it is I who take you that you would sit beside the still waters.

It is I who will take you that you would sit in peace in green pastures.

It is in the Spirit my son.

It is as you pray.

Jeff Lacki

It is as you empty yourself that the fullness comes upon you.

You are not empty my son, for it is I who am in you, my son.

These are my words to you:

Let there be peace that you would receive my peace.

Let there be peace my son that you would have faith - faith in Me, and knowledge that I am taking care of you.

Knowledge that I am with you my son, that I never leave you.

Let this peace be upon you.

Sit beside the still waters.

Listen to their beauty as they would flow by you.

Listen my son, and be at peace in your heart.

Be at peace in your mind.

Reflect upon things that are everlasting, and know my son, that it is these that are held within your hand.

It is these things that are yours my son, because I give them to you.

Let this be your peace.

Let this be your joy.

Let this be your faith my son, let it be your faith.

My son, many times in your life, many times, my son, I have taken you to a place.

A place of glory.

A place where wonderful things happen and yet it is a place of great sorrow, for many times, my son,

I would take you to the foot of my own Cross that there you might kneel, that there you might repent, *that there you might receive forgiveness, that there you might come to know Me and to know Me more, my son.*

Many times you have been at this place, and many times it has been in the sorrow of your heart, my son.

It has been in the great sorrow of your heart that you have knelt before the Cross.

But my son, it has not been sorrow for Me.

It has not been sorrow for what I endured or what I went through.

It is the sorrow of your own heart my son, for your eyes are upon yourself.

Your eyes are upon your own life, and so it is that I would take you to the Cross now and I would say:

"Lift up your eyes my son...Look upon the Cross."

I am not on the Cross my son.

I do not hang on the Cross, for truly I have been taken down from the Cross, and truly I have risen, and truly I am more than you think my son.

Truly I sit at the right hand of the Father and together we are as one.

Together we are as one and we rule over all things.

Lift your head, my son, and look upon the Cross.

For in this is your strength, in this is your hope.

Take your eyes off yourself, my son - Let your eyes be filled with Me.

Take your thoughts off yourself, my son - Let your mind be filled with Me.

Let your heart be filled with Me and let my Spirit

Jeff Lacki

come in my son, to every place that you hold dear, to every place that still you cling to.

It is mine, my son - I claim it.

And I desire it and I ask that you would let loose of it that I might come in my son, and still it is the Cross for you.

It is the Cross for you even as it was the Cross for Me my son.

This is a time for you that you would take your place on the Cross, that though you would see it as empty for I am not there, yet you would take your own place upon it.

And you would take your mind away from yourself, your thoughts away from yourself, your sorrow away from yourself.

Let it be filled instead with my thoughts...with my joy, my son.

These are my words to you:

It is the Cross for you, but it is in joy...it is in redemption...and truly it is in resurrection.

It is resurrection in your life my son.

These are my words, these are my words to you.

"It is Finished"

When Jesus spoke these words 2,000 years ago on the Cross, He spoke one of the most amazing things since Adam and Eve were created. Jesus was sent to Earth to redeem us from what Satan stole from each of us that day in the Garden. The Lord told Adam that He was giving him power and dominion over all the Earth: **Then God said, "Let us make man in our image, in our likeness, and let them rule over the fish of the sea and the birds of the air, over all the livestock, over all the earth, and over all the creatures that move along the ground" (Genesis 1:26).**

When they sinned by eating of the forbidden tree, they gave all power and authority to Satan over the Earth. All kinds of curses came upon the Earth and upon us as a result. The Bible is full of references to blessings and curses based on your obedience or disobedience to the Lord. I've listened to teachings on the theory that things like mosquitos, weeds, flies, and the nastier things on this planet were a result of the curse. They base this on the following scripture: **"Cursed is the ground because of you; through painful toil you will eat of it all the days of your life. It will produce thorns and thistles for you, and you will eat the plants of the field. By the sweat of your brow you will eat your food until you return to the ground, since from it you were taken; for dust you are and to dust you will return" (Genesis 3:17–19).** Even the Pharasees accused Jesus of being Beelzebub (which means Lord of the Flys), **"But when the Pharisees heard** this, they said, **"It is only by Beelzebub, the prince of demons, that this fellow drives out demons" (Matthew 12:24).** I cannot say for sure one way or the other as the Bible does not go into very much detail, but I can say that it is entirely possible. God is a God of goodness, not evil. Satan's kingdom is a kingdom of fear, torment, and control. The curses and things that happen that are bad in this world are a direct result of Satan's kingdom, not Gods lack of control as many suggest. If you read the Old Testament, particularly Deuteronomy, you will find the topic of curses all over.

Many people who do not know the Lord will argue that God created evil by the fact that Satan was created and is the head of evil in this world. They fail to realize that God gave each of us free will to do what we want during our lifetime. We can choose Him or choose Satan. When God created Satan and the other angels, He gave them freewill as well. Jesus says in **Matthew 12:30, "He who is not with me is against me, and he who does not gather with me scatters."** A persons' choice to *not* follow the Lord is already a choice *to* follow and help Satan, whether they believe in Satan or not. The Lord spoke to us one night at prayer about our choices and what we do with them:

My children, I would speak truth to you now my children that for every life, there is a path that you must walk, there is a journey that you would take.

And for each person, many times, there is a crossroad my children.

There is a place of decision.

You would take one way and it would not be right and you would take another, and yes, this is the right path, and though you would chose the right path once,

still there is a crossroad and still you must decide, or if you have made the wrong choice and down the wrong path you would go, still, I am merciful and I am kind and there is another crossroad for you my children.

Back on the right path, led back in the right direction, for this is the way my children, for all.

You have chosen right and you have chosen well, and yet, another decision is before you or you have chosen wrong and you have done poorly, and yet, another place that you would redeem yourself, for I have redeemed you my children.

This is the way of life.

Choose right paths my children, each time that you would come to a fork in the road.

Choose right paths my children, these are my words to you, that you would be humble in your lives, that you would be humble, and you would not walk boldly before Me, and you would not lag behind Me, but instead, in humility, your ears would open and you would seek Me in your heart.

Let your ears hear my children, let your eyes see, for I am before you and calling you and I will lead you on right paths my children, for truly, these are exciting times my children, these are great days in your life.

Choose right paths my children, for I will use you in your lives and you will change that which is around you.

You will change the hearts of people, for I will use you for my Kingdom.

These are my words my children, and is it not for good?

Is it not for my glory?

Is it not for my love, and should you not be excited in these things?

Be excited my children, for things are good as you choose right paths, as you make good decisions.

Choose the right path my children, as you would come to the fork in the road.

Choose the right path my children. I will make it easy for you.

Follow my voice my children, follow my voice.

We all know that we each will choose bad things at times and later regret those choices. After all, we all sin, no matter who we are or how closely we walk with the Lord. Often times we sin knowing that it is wrong, but our flesh desires it so much that we do it anyhow. This is our free will at work. Satan and his demons (fallen angels) chose to disobey and rebel against the Lord. God created them in purity and holiness in His own image, but they decided, in pride, that they were more powerful than the Lord. That's when God created hell to put Satan and the fallen angels (demons) for all eternity. Hell was never created for man. Satan's sole purpose is to take as many human beings to hell with him as he possibly can, because he knows how much God loves us. **John 10:10** says, **"The thief comes only to steal and kill and destroy; I have come that they may have life, and have it to the full."** What Satan cannot kill, he will steal from or destroy at *every* opportunity. Satan has stolen from each of us joy, peace, happiness, dreams, and ambitions. But Jesus came to give us back that which was stolen and lost. If there is *any* brokenness or hurt in your life, Satan will do his very best to exploit it and hurt you further. This often comes when someone else does something that triggers that hurting place in your life. Jesus came that you could be healed of those wounds caused by your enemy.

Jesus stated on the Cross that from this point on, all things that were once stolen from us by the fall in the Garden are now available to us again. The only thing is, it has to be our free will to accept it first. It is a *free* gift. Salvation is the first step. Once you are saved, this is only the beginning. It is as Solomon's temple described in the Bible in which you enter the outer courts at salvation time. As you walk with the Lord daily and over time, you move closer and closer to the most Holy of Holies in the inner sanctuary.

Jesus came to give us all things which are good. Not just salvation, but health, prosperity, peace, joy, happiness, and everything that is of love and goodness. Many will say, but I'm already saved, why don't I have those things? There are several reasons that may be causing them not to come to you. It may also be that the Lord is having you walk through a period of time in which He is testing you and trying you to make sure you will follow him obediently for greater use in His Kingdom. Later, after you have stood the test, He shall bless you far greater than you could have imagined. This is what has been going on in my life for nearly 7 years. I've been completely broke for quite a while, and at times unhealthy, oppressed, depressed, lonely, and without peace. But through each trial, God has never left me. He continues to encourage me to press on towards the prize He has for me. Don't get me wrong; it has not been easy! As I said earlier in this book, there is a cost to follow Christ, but it is well

worth it. I often gave power to my enemy by my own choices to not allow God's peace and joy to come over me. We must remember daily that we are in a battle to keep that which God has already given to us!

Many times I wanted to turn my back on God. I asked all the questions we all ask. "God why are you doing this to me? Why don't you answer my prayers? Where are you? Why are you allowing such deep loneliness and longing for another in my heart for so, so long?" I can't sit here and make it sound all rosy, because the honest truth is it was the hardest thing I've ever walked through in my entire life. What I can tell you is that when God's seasons of testing are over, there is joy and happiness that is surely coming to you if you don't give up! **Galations 6:9** says, **"Let us not become weary in doing good, for at the proper time we will reap a harvest if we do not give up."** Satan also knows this scripture and tries his best to make us give up before we receive our reward!

The Lord spoke this word to me once during a prayer meeting when I was at yet another low point in my walk with him and very discouraged:

My son, I speak truth to you.

Down through the ages there is a prayer that has been lifted to Me.

Over many years my church would pray, and the very words they would speak, they would negate their own prayer.

"If it be your will."

"If it be your will may I be healed."

"If it be your will may I be blessed."

"If it be your will may I prosper."

...If it be my will.

Can it be that my children would not know Me?

Can it be that there is such little faith that they would negate their own prayers?

If it be your will, let there be healing.

It is my will my son, it is always my will.

If it be your will, let there be prosperity.

My son, all that I have, I freely have given.

It is always my will.

Let there be faith my son, let your eyes be placed on Me, for this too is my will.

Do not step back, do not shrink my son before Me.

It is my desire that you would grow.

...If it be my will.

My son, all things that are good, they are my will.

All things prayed in my Spirit, truly it is my will.

Let your faith arise my son!

Let it be as the sun that would take its place in the sky!

Let it rise up!

Let the glory come forth!

Let it shine, for it is the faith that I have placed within you.

It is there my son, it is for you.

It is time to shine.

If it be my will...

My son, you have heard Me speak.

This is my will:

That you would prosper.

That you would be healed.

That you would know Me, my son.

This is my will.

Let it be done my son, according to my will.
Let it be done in you.
These are my words.
These are my words.

I spoke with a young lady online just last night as I was working on this book. In the course of the conversation, I found out she has had seizures for several years and taking medicine to control it. The Lord put on my heart to ask her more questions about this illness, as sometimes these things are caused by demonic forces. I was involved in a deliverance and healing ministry for four years, so I asked her some questions. I found out she was raped by her father when she was 6. He was a drug dealer as well. I told her I felt the seizures were a result of demonic entry during the rape, but had no specific word from God. I did feel that I had to share that with her though, and I did. She told me that she didn't really mind taking the 1.5 pills a day to control the seizures. She didn't see the need to look into it further because her life seemed ok, and she was dealing fine with it. I explained to her that Jesus came to free us from *every* disease and sickness and to deliver us. I also asked her why she would want any part of Satan in her life (if indeed this was not natural). She just said the same thing; it didn't bother her to take meds and she was fine with her life as it was.

I find it very hard to comprehend that we, as the Body of Christ, will tolerate any less than what Jesus came to give us on the Cross! I admit that I too at times will tolerate sin and ungodliness in my life due to my flesh. But at the core of it, I always ask God to deliver me and help me overcome my sinful desires. I don't want anything less than everything God came

to give me! I want to walk in victory, power, anointing, and everything else that the Lord has for me while I'm on this earth. I want to see as many souls saved from hell as possible. We are to be salt and light of the earth. Many people think that we need to tolerate sin around us, or they just don't care enough to pray and change this world for God. We are called to change this world, not let the world change us! Prayer is the key. We need to be in constant prayer day in and day out in our lives. It doesn't have to be on our knees and big, flowery prayers always. It is just communicating with God when we have the opportunity, whether driving, shopping, laying in bed trying to sleep, wherever and whenever–prayer is so important! **"The weapons we fight with are not the weapons of the world. On the contrary, they have divine power to demolish strongholds" (2Corinthians 10:4).**

Conclusion

As I sit here in my brand new home, God keeps reminding me that as we seek His kingdom and His righteousness, do the works He has prepared for us to do ahead of time, and remain in close relationship to Him, He does indeed bless us and give us the desires of our heart. It's a hard lesson to learn, but as we let our dreams die and say to the Lord, "I will follow you and do your will no matter what the cost," He will heal us, deliver us, and bring us the desires of our heart. I used to think that giving your heart to the Lord meant that you had to move and go into full time ministry. The truth is, God will use your talents, abilities and the things that you already desire to do in your heart for His purposes right where you are. The joy of doing it for Him and not for yourself far outweighs the momentary sufferings and trials we go through while we walk with Him. I didn't have to move to another country or give up anything of great value. Just like the Israelites for the 40 years in the desert, my clothes have not worn out. I was fed and sheltered each and every day. Looking back, why did I worry? God had a plan, even if I did not know it or see it. Many times I had to remind myself that today is the day that the Lord has made and given to me. I need to enjoy it for what it is. Take a bike ride, go for a drive, and live in freedom the way He has given it to me already, both in the natural and the spirit.

My greatest desire for this book is that it will touch many people's lives for His Kingdom. I did not want to put some things in this book, but the Lord

directed me to anyhow. My goal has not been to impress you by how great I am or how great God thinks of me, because honestly, I'm nobody, but He is everything! My goal was to demonstrate how great He is and how much He loves each of us even as we walk through this slowly deteriorating world of ours. I pray that it has helped you in knowing Him in a greater way and encourages you to press on and "fight the good fight of faith!" Remember to pray as often as possible. It's a very effective tool in our war!

May God bless you and keep you and make his Face to shine upon you, in Jesus Name!

My son, you stand on the mountain, and you would stand in strength and you would see all that is about you, you would see the beauty, you would know that it is Me my son and it would bring joy to your heart.

You would see the sun, and it is half behind the mountains and the sky is beautiful, for the clouds are reflecting the glory of the sun and there are many colors.

And you would see the beauty, it would bring tears to your eyes, for again you would know it is Me.

Even in this time my son, you would wonder:
Is the sun rising?
Is the sun setting?

You would not know and you would wonder my son, and I speak truth to you, be not confused my son, for truly it is the rising of the sun upon you.

Truly it is the coming of the light that you would stand in strength and you would have grown in Me my son.

You have prepared for the night and yet I will bring the day my son.

These are my words to you:

Hold on to your faith my son, hold on to your faith.

For those who have faith, I reward my son.

Those who have faith, I do not leave.

I will not abandon you to the night my son.

I will cause the sun to rise upon you.

I will cause the beauty to be all about you, and what you see obscured in darkness, for you would think the sun is setting, yet I am bringing the light.

You will see in clarity that which you have desired, that which you have seen in the half-light, you will see in the full light my son; for it is my desire that you would see it.

It is my desire that you would know, it is Me my son, in all things, it is Me.

Jeff Lacki

Salvation Prayer

If you have never prayed the salvation prayer, or if you have and have decided that today you want to re-dedicate your life to Jesus Christ, from your heart, pray this prayer. The Lord shall come into your heart and life right now, and you can know with certainty that you are His forever and ever and will be with Him in heaven when you die. You shall be "born again." God's free gift of salvation is not something you work towards by being good or cleaning up your life. Jesus meets you in your weakness and sinfulness, no matter what you have *ever* done, even murder and other detestable things! This free gift is for *everyone!* It is by His help you clean up your life and start a brand new life in Him.

Lord Jesus, please forgive me for my sins and my failures in the past. I realize now that I have been living my life apart from you and not following you as I was created to do. I repent of my former lifestyle, and by your help I will change and become the person you created me to be. Wash me in the blood of Jesus right now and make me as white as snow in your eyes. I believe now that all of my sins are forgiven and you will not count them against me any longer. I believe that you are the Son of the Living God. God the Father sent you to us as a man born of a virgin to the earth to suffer and die for my sins. You were then buried and after 3 days rose from the dead to sit at God's right hand. I now invite you into my heart to be my Lord and Savior from this point on. With your continued help I will try my best to walk in your ways and your commands. Please

teach me and show me the way to live and help me live this life for you. In Jesus name I pray, amen.

"If anyone is in Christ, he is a new creation; the old has gone, the new has come!" (2Corinthians 5:17). And **"Even to this day when Moses is read, a veil covers their hearts. But whenever anyone turns to the Lord, the veil is taken away" (2Corinthians 3:15–16).**

The very first person I led to the Lord had an interesting and probably common experience. As I was sharing the salvation message with her and how to receive it, a great oppression came over her. She even said it was slightly painful. I told her it was Satan trying to stop her from receiving Jesus because Satan knew he was about to lose her to the Lord. I prayed and bound that evil spirit, and she was able to continue to accept Jesus into her heart. Immediately, she said she felt the oppression leave her. A great peace and joy came over her. This is just one person's experience. My own experience was quite dull and uneventful. But I believe each person has their own experience with the Lord, even as we each have our own individuality and are unique as God has created us to be. Remember, Satan *will* try to stop you! After you pray this prayer, you may find that all of a sudden troubles and people will immediately start coming against you. It is because you no longer belong to this world, but to the Lord and Heaven forever and ever. As you are obedient and walk with God, also know that whatever happens from this point on does not happen by accident. It is allowed by God's filter of love for you as He grows you and strengthens you for the tasks ahead in these last days. There truly is no greater joy than helping others to come and grow

Jeff Lacki

in the Lord Jesus Christ! I still get a kick out of leading people to the truth. **"Then you will know the truth, and the truth will set you free" (John 8:32).** God bless you as you learn and grow in Him!

Contact Jeff Lacki
www.jefflacki.com

or order more copies of this book at

TATE PUBLISHING, LLC

127 East Trade Center Terrace
Mustang, OK 73064

(888) 361 - 9473

Tate Publishing, LLC

www.tatepublishing.com